T0334092

Cambridge Elements ≡

Elements in Eighteenth-Century Connections
edited by
Eve Tavor Bannet
University of Oklahoma
Markman Ellis
Queen Mary University of London

MAKING BOSWELL'S *LIFE* *OF JOHNSON*

An Author-Publisher and His Support Network

Richard B. Sher
New Jersey Institute of Technology/ Rutgers University, Newark

CAMBRIDGE
UNIVERSITY PRESS

CAMBRIDGE
UNIVERSITY PRESS

Shaftesbury Road, Cambridge CB2 8EA, United Kingdom

One Liberty Plaza, 20th Floor, New York, NY 10006, USA

477 Williamstown Road, Port Melbourne, VIC 3207, Australia

314–321, 3rd Floor, Plot 3, Splendor Forum, Jasola District Centre, New Delhi – 110025, India

103 Penang Road, #05–06/07, Visioncrest Commercial, Singapore 238467

Cambridge University Press is part of Cambridge University Press & Assessment, a department of the University of Cambridge.

We share the University's mission to contribute to society through the pursuit of education, learning and research at the highest international levels of excellence.

www.cambridge.org
Information on this title: www.cambridge.org/9781009271424

DOI: 10.1017/9781009271431

First published 2023

A catalogue record for this publication is available from the British Library.

ISBN 978-1-009-27142-4 Paperback
ISSN 2632-5578 (online)
ISSN 2632-556x (print)

Making Boswell's *Life of Johnson*

An Author-Publisher and His Support Network

Elements in Eighteenth-Century Connections

DOI: 10.1017/9781009271431
First published online: July 2023

Richard B. Sher
New Jersey Institute of Technology/Rutgers University, Newark
Author for correspondence: Richard B. Sher, sher@njit.edu

Abstract: This Element throws new light on James Boswell's *Life of Samuel Johnson* by investigating its early publication history. Despite precarious psychological and financial circumstances and other limitations, Boswell was both author and publisher of the two-volume quarto edition that appeared in 1791. This study utilizes little-known documents to explore the details and implications of Boswell's risky undertaking. It argues that the success of the first edition was the result not only of Boswell's biographical genius but also of collaboration with a devoted support network, including the bookseller Charles Dilly, the printer Henry Baldwin and his employees, several newspaper and magazine editors, Boswell's "Gang" (Edmond Malone, Sir Joshua Reynolds, and John Courtenay) and other members of The Club, and Sir William Forbes. Although the muddled second edition (1793) suffered from Boswell's increasing dysfunction in the years before his death in 1795, the resilient Boswellian network subsequently secured the book's exalted reputation.

Keywords: James Boswell, Samuel Johnson, *Life of Samuel Johnson*, support network, author-publisher

ISBNs: 9781009271424 (PB), 9781009271431 (OC)
ISSNs: 2632-5578 (online), 2632-556x (print)

Contents

1 Introduction

James Boswell's *The Life of Samuel Johnson* has been a source of fascination ever since its publication in 1791. Rarely has someone dominated the literary life of a time and place as thoroughly as Samuel Johnson did in London during his mature years, from the mid-eighteenth century until his death in 1784. The range of his publications was extensive: *The Rambler* (1750–2), *The Idler* (1758–60), and other periodical essays; a colossal *Dictionary of the English Language* (1755); *Rasselas*, a popular work of fiction (1759); an edition of *The Plays of William Shakespeare* (1765); an account of a tour of Scotland with Boswell titled *A Journey to the Western Islands of Scotland* (1775); a series of biographical prefaces to a multivolume poetry anthology (1779–81), later published separately as *Lives of the English Poets*; and much more. Yet Boswell had no intention of writing an intellectual biography, and his book would have relatively little to say about the substance of Johnson's published works. Rather, his aim was to capture what he called Johnson's "character," ascertained less from his publications than from his correspondence and conversation.

In the opening pages, Boswell stated that "the conversation of a celebrated man, if his talents have been exerted in conversation, will best display his character" (*Life*, 1:31). From their first meeting in May 1763, when he was just twenty-two years old and Johnson fifty-three, Boswell revered Johnson and sought to spend as much time with him as he could, acquiring "a facility in recollecting," and being "very assiduous in recording, his conversation, of which the extraordinary vigour and vivacity constituted one of the first features of his character" (*Life*, 1:26). As a Scot practicing law in Edinburgh, however, he had limited opportunities to be with Johnson – usually on annual visits to London in late winter and early spring, augmented by occasional meetings and travels elsewhere in England, and their excursion to the Hebrides in 1773. Nevertheless, Boswell claimed that by tracing his subject's correspondence and conversation chronologically he could produce a biography "more lively, and will make my readers better acquainted with him, than even most of those were who actually knew him, but could know him only partially." Indeed, he boasted that his method would enable Johnson to be seen "as he really was," and "more completely than any man who has ever yet lived" (*Life*, 1:29–30).

The main materials for learning how Boswell attempted to achieve this ambitious goal were discovered in two stages during the first half of the twentieth century (Buchanan, 1974; Pottle, 1982). First, in the 1920s an enormous fund of documents, including most of Boswell's journal (later supplemented by most of the manuscript of the *Life of Johnson*), emerged unexpectedly from Malahide Castle in Ireland. From this find came an eighteen-volume, privately printed edition of Boswell's *Private Papers* edited by Geoffrey Scott and Frederick Pottle (Scott & Pottle, 1928–34), who also produced a thorough bibliography of Boswell's publications during this period (Pottle, 1929). Then a second large collection of Boswell manuscripts, mostly correspondence, surfaced at Fettercairn House in Scotland during the 1930s. From the middle of the twentieth century, most of the materials from these two remarkable discoveries found a home at the Beinecke Rare Book and Manuscript Library at Yale University and became increasingly accessible through volumes published in the Yale Editions of the Private Papers of James Boswell. Landmarks for the *Life of Johnson* include the trade edition of Boswell's journal in thirteen volumes (1950–89, esp. Lustig & Pottle, 1986, and Danziger & Brady, 1989); the comprehensive catalogue of the Boswell papers at Yale (Pottle, Abbott & Pottle, 1993); Marshall Waingrow's masterful compilation of relevant correspondence, first published in 1969 (Waingrow, 2001); and the monumental four-volume manuscript edition of the *Life* (Waingrow, 1994; Redford with Goldring, 1998; Bonnell, 2012, 2019). Biographies of Boswell's earlier and later years (Pottle, 1966; Brady, 1984) were also part of the Yale project.

Thanks to these works and others, and to the recent digitization of much of the unpublished Boswell material at Yale, it has become possible to see how Boswell sought out and recorded Johnson's conversation, obtained and applied other materials, crafted the manuscript of the text from the entries in his journal, his correspondence, and other sources and then – working closely with his frequent collaborator Edmond Malone – transformed the work, through rigorous and often creative revisions, from manuscript to proofs to published book. Engaging with this process reveals the complexity and artfulness of the *Life* (Waingrow, 2001, p. xxvi; Redford, 2002). Gone was the nineteenth-century view of Boswell as a mere transcriber of Johnson's words – "the reporter Boswell," in Geoffrey Scott's dismissive phrase (Scott & Pottle, 1928–34, 6:30). Rather, it became clear that the depictions of Johnson's conversation in the *Life* were based on entries recorded in Boswell's journal but were altered for various purposes, such as making the text more concise and readable, rendering scenes more dramatic, and showing certain individuals in a better (or worse) light, or sometimes concealing their identities entirely. Moreover, it was learned that material taken from the journal constitutes less than half of the book. For the rest, Boswell had to go elsewhere, and so must scholars. As Marshall Waingrow put it, "for a complete history of the *Life of Johnson* it is necessary to look beyond the journal and behind the manuscript: specifically, at that part of the making of the *Life* which cast Boswell in the roles of researcher, compiler, and editor" (Waingrow, 2001, pp. xxv–xxvi).

The fundamental premise of this study is that "a complete history of the *Life of Johnson*" also requires careful assessment of another of Boswell's roles, which has largely eluded scholarly analysis: the role of author-publisher. This term draws attention to the fact that Boswell did not merely write the *Life of Johnson*; he was also chiefly responsible for publishing it. During the eighteenth century, especially its last decades, thousands of British books contained the phrase "Printed for the Author" on their title pages (Downie, 2013, p. 74). Those words indicated that the author covered the expenses of production and promotion and owned the product, both materially (the printed copies) and abstractly (the copyright). To facilitate this process, a circular issued by one enterprising London bookseller announced that "Authors who retain their own Copy Right, may have their Books published in London for a small Commission" (Hamilton & Company, 1794). Subscription publishing was another option for authors wishing to publish their own works, and various hybrid options were also available (Sher, 2006, pp. 224–35; Downie, 2013, pp. 64, 70). Yet it is unlikely that most authors of self-published books were as deeply engaged in the publication process as Boswell. Although the phrase "Printed for the Author" does not appear in the imprint of the *Life of Johnson*, Boswell not only assumed full financial responsibility but also made decisions about all aspects of production, participated in selling the book, wrote advertising copy, and received all the publishing profits. He was therefore an author-publisher in the fullest sense of that term.

At the turn of this century, Adam Sisman produced a lucid narrative about the making of the *Life of Johnson* based on Boswell's published journal and correspondence as well as other published sources (Sisman, 2002, p. xx). This Element seeks to dig deeper. In addition to the materials Sisman used, and others published since his book appeared, this study relies heavily on underutilized older published sources, such as contemporary articles and advertisements in newspapers and periodicals, unpublished correspondence, and book trade documents that have never been published or digitized and have rarely been consulted by scholars. The most important of these documents is a complete impression account of the first edition of the *Life*, located among the Boswell Papers at the Beinecke Library (Yale, A 59). Unlike printing ledgers, which normally do not contain information about paper, advertising, and other matters, an impression account (the complete record of a bibliographical "impression") contains details about all aspects of an edition. Another neglected item in the Beinecke Library is a summary of the printing and paper charges for the first edition. Sales records for the first and second (1793) editions have also survived, as have Boswell's notes about anticipated costs and profits from the second edition (Yale, A 60–64). Furthermore, an impression account of the posthumous third edition of 1799, incorporating the printing record, is among the papers of the executor of Boswell's estate – Boswell's Edinburgh banker and confidante, Sir William Forbes of Pitsligo – in the National Library of Scotland. The wealth of information that these materials provide about the making of the *Life of Johnson* is exceptional for an eighteenth-century book. Used in conjunction with other sources, they throw new light on the early editions.

In this Element, the primary device for making sense of these neglected materials, and for bringing new meaning to traditional sources, is the concept of the support network. We shall see that in making the *Life of Johnson*, Boswell relied on several kinds of overlapping networks, predominantly male and almost entirely situated in London. They included a social club and a more intimate literary coterie within it, a London bookseller, a printer and the workers in his shop, several newspaper and periodical editors and printers, an adviser in Edinburgh, some family members, and a correspondence network of friends, acquaintances, and well-meaning readers who made contributions to the book. The relationships that characterized these networks were at once personal and professional, intellectual and commercial. These interlocking networks enabled Boswell to publish, promote, and revise his biography of Johnson despite various disadvantages and disabilities, and they continued to drive the book's success after Boswell's death. Taken together, they constitute what I am calling Boswell's support network.

With sensitivity to the complexities and contingencies that lie between a manuscript text and a published book, and between one edition of a book and another, this study probes the publication history of the early editions of the *Life of Johnson* by means of these concepts and materials. It argues that (1) the first edition of 1791 was a successful blend of art and enterprise, in which a highly motivated but in some ways flawed author-publisher made a series of wise publishing decisions with the help of his devoted support network; (2) the second edition of 1793 constituted a setback for the book, as an increasingly dysfunctional author-publisher, relying less on his support network, made a number of poor decisions, resulting in a publication that was deficient in several respects; and (3) beginning with the posthumous third edition of 1799, and continuing through the ninth edition of 1822, the extraordinarily resilient and dedicated remnant of the author's support network, backed from 1803 by Britain's foremost publishing and bookselling firm, enhanced and expanded the book while staying true to the author's text and original vision, in the process establishing the work's reputation as a biographical masterpiece.

1.1 "At His Own Risque"

When the *Life of Johnson* appeared in London on 16 May 1791, the imprint on the title page announced in capital letters "PRINTED BY HENRY BALDWIN, FOR

CHARLES DILLY, IN THE POULTRY" (Figures 1a & 1b) – the same wording that six years earlier had graced the title page of Boswell's first Johnsonian volume, *The Journal of a Tour to the Hebrides, with Samuel Johnson* (hereafter cited as *Tour*). Upon seeing that imprint, which contained the standard terminology for identifying a book's printer ("printed by") and publisher ("printed for"), a reader would naturally assume that Charles Dilly was the sole publisher and that Boswell had either sold the copyright to him outright or else made a conditional arrangement to receive half the profits, as was commonly done (Raven, 2007, p. 333). In his career as a publishing bookseller, Dilly made use of both these methods, though his preference was for profit-sharing (Sher, 2006, p. 348). How, then, did the *Life of Johnson* come to be published by Boswell, and what was the significance of the arrangement with Dilly?

In August 1767 Edward and Charles Dilly agreed to pay Boswell one hundred guineas (£105) for the copyright to his first major book, *An Account of Corsica*. Printed in Glasgow by Robert and Andrew Foulis and published in February 1768 as a six-shilling octavo (Boswell, 1768; Gaskell, 1986, pp. 278–79, 396–400), it was hugely successful in promoting the ill-fated cause of Corsican independence under General Pasquale Paoli and brought "Corsica Boswell" an international reputation (Pottle, 1929, pp. 50–75; Pottle, 1966, pp. 237–39, 354, 364–68). It also established a strong connection with the Dilly brothers, who "thought they could not do enough for me," as Boswell wrote in his journal on 1 September 1769. Boswell grew especially close with Charles Dilly after Edward died in 1779. In the mid-1780s, when Boswell was contemplating publishing the journal of his excursion to the Hebrides with Johnson, he proposed to Dilly, in a letter of 23 December 1784 which has not survived but was summarized in Boswell's register of correspondence, that they "go halves in an edition" (Yale, M 255). Dilly's reply of 29 January 1785 is also known only from Boswell's summary: "Mr. C. Dilly ... wishes me to have all the profits of my Tour to the Hebrides, & he will be the Publisher" (Yale, M 255). That is, Dilly would manage the publication in exchange for a commission, and his name would appear on the title page as if he were the publisher.

Dilly extended similarly favorable terms to the *Life of Johnson*, for which he would receive 7½ percent of gross wholesale income as a commission. I have been unable to determine if 7½ percent was a standard commission or a discounted rate for Boswell's benefit. In 1816 the standard bookseller's commission in London was 10 percent (Downie, 2013, p. 66), but that rate may reflect an increase occurring throughout the trade. Registrations at Stationers' Hall – a necessary step to protect a book from piracy within Great Britain – reflect the changes in Boswell and Dilly's publishing arrangements. Whereas the *Account of Corsica* was registered on 15 February 1768 to "Edwd & Charles Dilly," the *Life* was registered on 11 May 1791

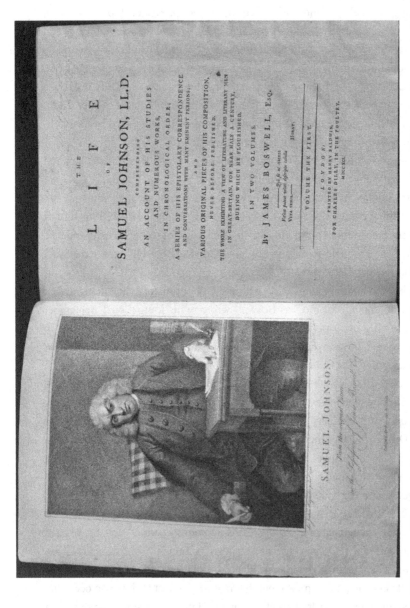

Figure 1a Title page of the quarto first edition, opposite James Heath's frontispiece engraving of Johnson after a portrait by Sir Joshua Reynolds, "From the original Picture / in the Possession of James Boswell Esq." Terry I. Seymour Collection.

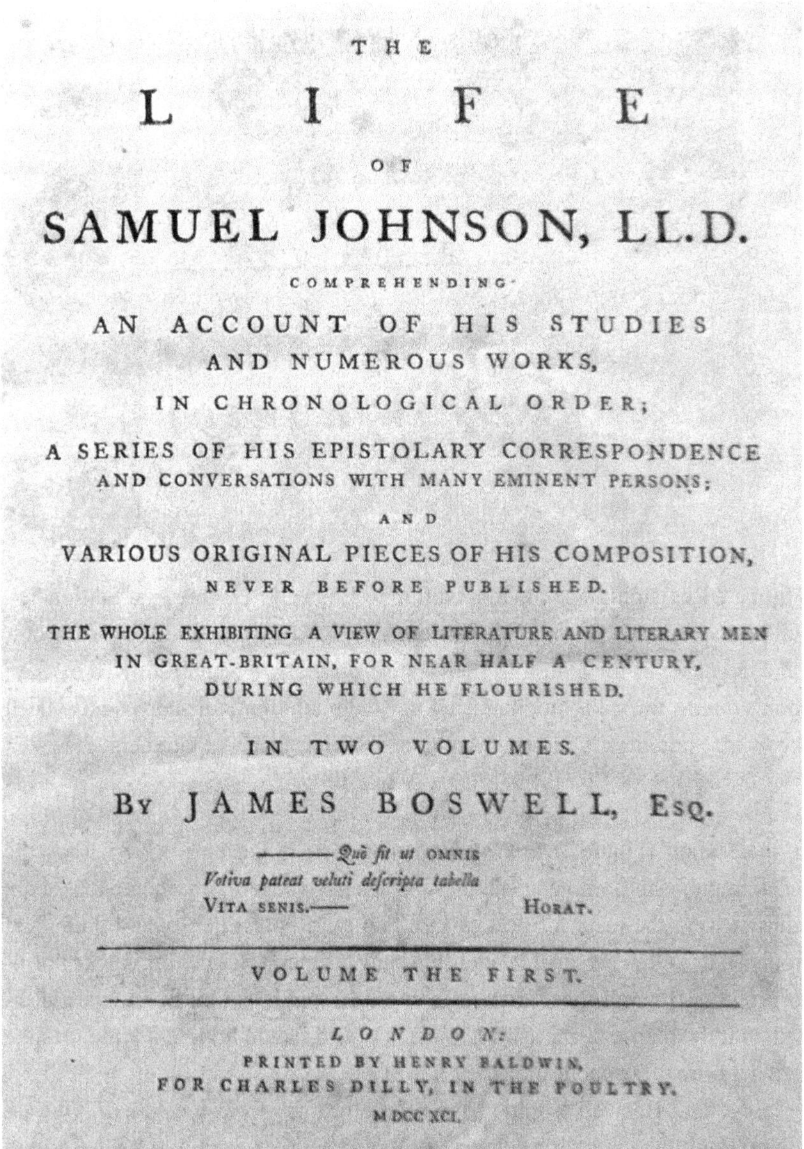

THE

L I F E

OF

SAMUEL JOHNSON, LL.D.

COMPREHENDING

AN ACCOUNT OF HIS STUDIES
AND NUMEROUS WORKS,

IN CHRONOLOGICAL ORDER;

A SERIES OF HIS EPISTOLARY CORRESPONDENCE
AND CONVERSATIONS WITH MANY EMINENT PERSONS;

AND

VARIOUS ORIGINAL PIECES OF HIS COMPOSITION,
NEVER BEFORE PUBLISHED.

THE WHOLE EXHIBITING A VIEW OF LITERATURE AND LITERARY MEN
IN GREAT-BRITAIN, FOR NEAR HALF A CENTURY,
DURING WHICH HE FLOURISHED.

IN TWO VOLUMES.

BY JAMES BOSWELL, ESQ.

———— *Quò fit ut* OMNIS
Votiva pateat veluti defcripta tabella
VITA SENIS.———— HORAT.

VOLUME THE FIRST.

LONDON:
PRINTED BY HENRY BALDWIN,
FOR CHARLES DILLY, IN THE POULTRY.
M DCC XCI.

Figure 1b Detail of the title page of the first edition from Figure 1a. Terry I.
Seymour Collection.

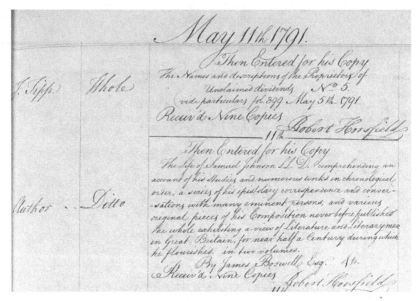

Figure 2 Registration of the first edition to Boswell ("Author") at Stationers'
Hall, London, on 11 May 1791. The entry reproduces the full title of the book
and the name of the author as they appear on the title page, followed by the
book's quarto format ("4to.") and acknowledgment that nine copies have been
received. Stationers' Company Archive, TSC/1/E/0611 – Stationers' Register
1786–1792, f. 400

to "the Author" (Figure 2), as the *Tour* had been on 28 September 1785. Thus, the
generous publishing arrangements that characterized both of Boswell's books about
Johnson were the result of acts of kindness by a bookseller toward an author,
grounded in a close personal relationship between them. Besides ceding the potential profits to Boswell, these arrangements would spare Boswell any stigma associated with the phrase "Printed for the Author" and would bring Dilly the prestige
deriving from these publications.

To say that Boswell would "have all the profits" from the *Life of Johnson*
presents only one side of the story. One could just as easily say that Boswell
would have all the losses. Another of Dilly's Scottish authors, the poet and
philosophy professor James Beattie, went to the heart of the matter when he
reported to a friend on 30 June 1791 that Boswell "publishes at his own risque"
(Fettercairn Papers, box 92). An author-publisher could reap large profits from
a book, but substantial financial losses were also possible, and the stakes
increased in proportion to a book's size and special features. The *Tour* was
a one-volume octavo of 535 total pages without any special features except an
inexpensive woodcut of Boswell's family crest on the title page (Baker, 1986,

Figure 3 The two-volume quarto first edition of the *Life of Johnson* (1791); the thin quarto *Principal Corrections and Additions to the First Edition* (1793); the three-volume octavo second edition (1793); one of the three volumes of the Dublin octavo edition (1792); the one-volume octavo first edition of the *Tour* (1785). Terry I. Seymour Collection

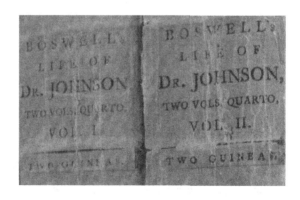

Figure 4 On the left is the first edition in boards, as it might be sold in bookshops. A purchaser might then pay a bookbinder to have the volumes bound in leather, as in Figure 3. On the right is a detail of the labels, showing the abbreviated title, number of volumes per set, format, volume number, and price. Beinecke Rare Book and Manuscript Library, Yale University

p. 199); it retailed for six shillings in boards – a rudimentary form of binding that was often preliminary to more expensive leather and gilt-tooled covers, such as those shown in Figure 3 (Hill, 1999). At that low price for such a thick volume, it was very good value, but the profit margin was consequently extremely thin, probably yielding no more than a few hundred pounds in combined publishing profits from the first two editions of 1,500 and 1,000 copies. Moreover, Boswell must have lost money on the sluggish third edition of 1786, illustrating the risks involved when authors published their own works.

The *Life of Johnson* was a different kind of undertaking. Published in two commodious volumes in the large and expensive quarto format, with various extra features that are discussed in this work, the first edition was much costlier to produce, seven times more expensive to buy at two guineas (£2 2s.) per set in boards (Figure 4), and a much riskier publishing endeavor than the *Tour*. Such a book could earn £1,000 or more – the equivalent of more than 150,000 British pounds or American dollars today. However, it could also lose large amounts. London's leading publisher of the mid-eighteenth century, Andrew Millar, once revealed to a contemporary that "he had lost by many more publications than he had gained" (quoted in Sher, 2006, p. 282).

A high level of risk brought correspondingly high levels of anxiety. As the author-publisher, Boswell had to make choices about every aspect of the production process, and every choice had financial implications. A notice appended to the first and second editions of the *Tour* referred to the forthcoming *Life of Johnson* as a "one Volume Quarto." As his text kept growing, Boswell had to decide whether he could afford to make the *Life* a two-volume quarto – or perhaps even a one-volume folio, as he once suggested. Other decisions were equally important. What paper and type should be used? Should the book contain illustrations, and if so, what kind, how many, and by whom? Should there be an index? How many copies should be printed, and how many should he take for his own use and for gifts? Before considering how Boswell answered such questions, it will be useful to investigate the network of knowledgeable and trustworthy individuals to whom he turned for guidance and support.

1.2 Boswell's Gendered, Anglicized Support Network

In recent years, much has been published about intellectual, social, and correspondence networks among men and women of letters in eighteenth-century Europe (e.g., Baird, 2014; Edmondson & Edelstein, 2019) and beyond (e.g., Gies & Wall, 2018; Czennia & Clingham, 2021, esp. p. 28 n. 27). Philosophes, literati, academicians, professors, and students associated in person, as did participants in literary and scientific clubs and societies, salons, coffee houses, masonic lodges, and places of worship. Private correspondences, circulating manuscripts, and a flood of printed materials – increasingly accessible in book clubs and lending libraries – linked individuals and groups and disseminated knowledge and ideas across geographical boundaries. Books played a central role in this process, and various kinds of commercial networks contributed to their production, distribution, and consumption (e.g., Darnton, 1979, and later works; Feather, 1985; Amory & Hall, 2000; Suarez & Turner, 2009; Gross & Kelley, 2010; Brown & McDougall, 2012; Hinks & Feely, 2017). There is also a growing literature about different varieties of readers, their institutions, and their "networks of improvement" (e.g., Mee, 2015; Towsey, 2019). However, it is not always clear how such diverse networks can be brought together to tell the story of a book.

As a result of his personality and circumstances, Boswell required a great deal of support to write and publish a book as large and complex as the *Life of Johnson*. He was prone to bouts of depression, alternating with periods of high exuberance – often resembling what might now be termed bipolar disorder (Purdie & Gow, 2002, p. 201). In a letter of 5 March 1791, his friend Malone attributed his condition to an "almost uniform intemperance in wine" and remarked that "the sure consequence of wild and intemperate riot for one half the year, must be the lowest depression during the other" (Baker, 1986, pp. 408–9). Alcohol abuse was certainly a problem for Boswell, especially late in life, but his psychological problems ran deeper. Boswell described his condition in a letter written seven months after publication of the *Life*, when he referred to the "alternate agitation and depression of spirits to which I am unhappily subject" (quoted in Brady, 1984, p. 458). A second disadvantage facing Boswell was that his financial circumstances were, as he sometimes put it, "embarrassed," especially after his permanent move to London in 1786. His transition from the Scottish to the English bar did not go well, and he struggled from a distance with the management of Auchinleck, his ancestral estate in Ayrshire. After the death of his wife, Margaret, from consumption (tuberculosis) in 1789, he was the widowed father of five young children, inclined to worsen his financial circumstances by borrowing more heavily. A third problem was his rudimentary understanding of book publishing. He loved books but, like most authors, had a limited grasp of formats, types, print runs, and other aspects of the trade.

Owing in large part to his skill at building and maintaining personal relationships, Boswell could rely on the assistance of loyal friends and supporters and skilled bookmen. Prominent among them were Charles Dilly, the bookseller who coordinated the production and distribution of the *Life*; the printer Henry Baldwin, who was closely associated with Dilly; and Edmond Malone, the Shakespeare scholar who had grown friendly with Boswell while helping to put the *Tour* through the press in 1785 and continued to work closely with him on the *Life*. These three men were devoted to Boswell, as he was to them. When

Boswell was considering an alternative publishing arrangement for the *Life*, as discussed in the next section, he wrote tellingly in his journal on 20 February 1791, "I was unwilling to separate myself as an Authour from Dilly, with whom my name had been so long connected." Boswell was also aided by others affiliated with the book and periodical trades, such as "my steady friend Mr. Isaac Reed" and "My worthy friend, Mr. John Nichols" (*Life*, 4:37, 244 n. 2; Hart, 1952; Pooley, 2011), who had provided an early warning against selling the copyright of the *Life* prematurely, as Boswell recorded in his journal on 29 May 1785. One of the two major engravings in the book owed much to the distinguished portrait painter Sir Joshua Reynolds – to whom the *Life* was dedicated in an adoring five-page tribute – as the other major engraving did to Sir William Forbes. To fill in the large gaps in his knowledge of the subject of his biography, Boswell depended heavily on Johnson's old friends.

Before and after publication, Boswell publicized himself and the *Life of Johnson* tirelessly, and often shamelessly, taking advantage of the fact that several of the most popular newspapers and magazines were in friendly hands: the *Gentleman's Magazine* (Nichols), *European Magazine* (Reed), *Public Advertiser* (Henry Sampson Woodfall), and *St. James's Chronicle* (Baldwin). The *St. James's Chronicle* was then edited by a young barrister working in Baldwin's shop as a press corrector, Thomas Edlyne Tomlins, who penned a favorable review of the *Life* that appeared on the day it was published (Yale, P 100.1 [1]; Pottle, Abbott & Pottle, 1993, 3:1066). Boswell benefited greatly from the services of others in Baldwin's shop, as well as from engravers and copperplate printers elsewhere in London. Family members assisted in various ways: Boswell's brother David (T. D.) provided an account of Johnson's death (*Life*, 4:417–18), while Margaret and several of their children – including precocious young James, who would become Malone's disciple as a Shakespeare editor – sometimes served as copyists (e.g., Yale, M 145). Several friends helped financially. The London booksellers did their part by purchasing large numbers of copies at Dilly and Boswell's trade sale. Friends and readers provided new materials, corrections, and suggestions, leading Boswell to assert in the introduction to the *Life* that such "communications" had given him "more advantages" than all but a few other biographers (*Life*, 1:26). Some people who assisted Boswell with the first edition also helped with the second edition of 1793, the posthumous third edition of 1799, and early nineteenth-century editions. In this way, Boswell's support network outlived Boswell himself.

The overwhelmingly male character of Boswell's support network reflects the homosocial literary world in which Boswell and Johnson usually traveled, most famously at The Club (or Literary Club) that Reynolds founded in 1764 as a service to Johnson. Election to The Club in 1773 was one of the high points of Boswell's life, and he often attended its meetings when he was in London. The Club was in some respects what Betty Schellenberg has termed a *"literary coterie"*: "a select group of individuals linked by ties of friendship founded upon, or deepened by, mutual encouragement to original composition" in manuscript and print, as well as "criticism of one another's work and of shared reading materials" (Schellenberg, 2016, p. 2). One example of it functioning this way is a letter from Johnson to Reynolds of 16 May 1776 about Johnson's draft of a Latin epitaph for a deceased member, Oliver Goldsmith: "Read it first yourself, and if You then think it right, show it to the Club" (Redford, 1992–4, 2:330). Members of The Club walked as a group in the funeral processions for its most eminent figures, such as Johnson and Reynolds, and Boswell turned to several members for information and assistance when writing his biography. Yet The Club was too diverse to be considered a literary coterie in the fullest sense of Schellenberg's definition. Its membership included a rival biographer of Johnson, Sir John Hawkins, and several individuals with whom Boswell did not always have mutually supportive relationships, notably Edmund Burke, with whom his interactions were often strained (Lambert, 1998); Edward Gibbon, whom he disliked for being "a notorious infidel" (*Life*, 3:409); Thomas Percy, Bishop of Dromore, whose relationship with Boswell deteriorated over the latter's refusal to alter certain passages about him in the *Life*; and the cantankerous Shakespeare scholar George Steevens, who sometimes boosted but also undermined Boswell's book (Tankard, 2012, p. 88).

There was, however, a four-man subset of The Club that more closely approximates Schellenberg's conception of a literary coterie. It consisted of Boswell, Reynolds, Malone, and John Courtenay, a late addition to The Club in 1788 who had helped Boswell and Malone with problems involving hostile reactions to the *Tour*. Courtenay used his office as an MP to give Boswell free postage by means of the controversial practice of parliamentary franking and was also helpful in other ways, especially while Malone was in Dublin from late autumn 1790 to spring 1791. These four became so close, and were so often together in the years leading up to publication of the *Life*, that one outsider christened them "the Gang" – an epithet that Boswell readily embraced (Sher, 2022, pp. 85 and 87 n. 3). Although differing politically (Courtenay a Foxite Whig, Boswell and Malone devout Tories, Reynolds unaffiliated), generationally (Reynolds, born in 1723, being fifteen to eighteen years older than the other three), and in their places of origin (Malone and Courtenay from Ireland, Boswell from Scotland, Reynolds from Devon in southwest England), they were mutually supportive. They shared a deep admiration for Johnson and a desire to see him portrayed sympathetically and brought to life more vigorously than in Hawkins's biography, which Boswell considered dull and "uncharitable" (*Life*, 1:28). They were also available: Reynolds and Malone were bachelors, and Courtenay looked for excuses to escape his large family. In 1789, as Boswell struggled with the death of his wife and Reynolds dealt with the loss of an eye (and therefore his career as a painter), "the Gang" rallied in support, as they also did when Reynolds needed their help to maintain the presidency of the Royal Academy of Arts in February and March 1790 (Sher, 2022, appendix 4). In short, "the Gang" was an intimate and dedicated social and literary support group that Boswell depended on as he prepared the *Life of Johnson* for the press.

Women were not entirely absent from the literary universe that Johnson and Boswell inhabited, and a few (e.g., Mary Adey and Lucy Porter) were among Boswell's informants. Female participation in the Boswellian network was limited, however, by its core attitudes toward Johnson and women. Frances Burney left two accounts (both in Larsen, 2008, pp. 151–55) of her resistance to Boswell's heavy-handed entreaties to obtain Johnson's letters to her. Among the women who did provide Boswell with material on Johnson were two, Anna Seward and Hester Lynch Thrale (Mrs. Piozzi from the time of her second marriage in July 1784), with whom his relations worsened over time for much the same reason: they were both more critical of Johnson than Boswell and "the Gang" would allow. Boswell dismissed their testimonies in a patronizing manner. In 1786–7 he met Seward's public (though thinly pseudonymous) criticisms in the *Gentleman's Magazine* of his portrayal of Johnson in the *Tour* with disdain. He was more brutally dismissive in his response to "the fair Lady," "my fair antagonist," "our poetess," and a member of "a cabal of minor poets and poetesses" in his acrimonious exchanges with Seward in the *Gentleman's Magazine* in late 1793 and early 1794 (in which Seward classified him among Johnson's "blind idolaters") over his refusal to include her unflattering anecdotes about Johnson in his biography (Kairoff, 2012, pp. 240–65; Serrat, 2019). Boswell's bad relations with Piozzi, Johnson's close friend until her second marriage brought about a rupture, began when she denied the story in the *Tour* that neither she nor Johnson could "get through" a book on Shakespeare by the prominent Bluestocking Elizabeth Montagu (*Life*, 5:245 & n. 2; Montagu, 1769; Lustig, 1972, pp. 26–28). Their relationship worsened after Piozzi publicized Johnson's faults in her *Anecdotes of the Late Samuel Johnson*, published in March 1786. Malone and Courtenay worked with Boswell to counterattack against Piozzi in the press and in the third edition of the *Tour* (McGowan, 1996, pp. 141–42). The lengthy strictures on Piozzi toward the end of the *Life* are unusually harsh, thanks largely to notes provided by an "eminent critick" – that is, Malone (*Life*, 4:339–47, quoting 341). Those strictures would have been still more severe if Courtenay had not gone to Boswell's home on the night of 22 February 1791 "and obligingly assisted me in *lightening* my animadversions on Mrs. Piozzi in my Life of Johnson – for my own credit." Boswell used gendered language in his journal to describe Courtenay's assistance on that occasion: "His manly mind conveyed to me some sympathetick force" (see also Lustig, 1972, pp. 20–23).

A poetic celebration of Johnson by Courtenay, published by Charles Dilly in early April 1786 as *A Poetical Review of the Literary and Moral Character of the Late Samuel Johnson*, reveals much about "the Gang." The poem cites Reynolds, Malone, and several other members of The Club among Johnson's "brilliant school," adding

> Amid these names can BOSWELL be forgot,
> Scarce by North Britons now esteem'd a Scot?
> Who to the sage devoted from his youth,
> Imbib'd from him the sacred love of truth;
> The keen research, the exercise of mind,
> And that best art, the art to know mankind. (Courtenay 1786a, pp. 22–24)

On one level, this tribute to Boswell was meant to promote the second edition of the *Tour*, which was then under attack from critics, and to set the stage for the promised *Life*. To this end, it stressed Boswell's devotion to Johnson and the traits he had learned from him: "love of truth," research skills, mental powers, and knowledge of "mankind." The passage and the poem were also a display of group solidarity and friendship by the younger members of "the Gang." As Courtenay was composing the poem with the help of Malone, a draft was shown to Boswell, who remarked to Malone on 24 January that "Courtenay's elogium ... elevated me much. It is beyond my warmest expectation. How much am I obliged to him." On 8 March Boswell, Malone, and Courtenay discussed the evolving text over dinner, and eight days later Malone and Courtenay revised the poem again (Baker, 1986, pp. 287–88, 292, 296, 301–2). It is not too much to say that Malone, and to a lesser extent Boswell, were "virtual co-authors" of Courtenay's poem (Redford, 2002, p. 61).

"Courtenay's elogium" also displays a national component in Boswell's support network. As outsiders to England, the younger members of "the Gang" all strove to assimilate. When Courtenay was writing his *Poetical Review* early in 1786, Boswell was about to make the biggest move of his life by leaving Edinburgh and relocating himself (and later in the year his whole family) in London. Three months after his move, the opening couplet in Courtenay's passage about him prompted Boswell to state in a newspaper that he considered these lines a "compliment": "The import of it is, that Mr. Boswell does not live solely with his countrymen in London; has not that narrow *nationality* [i.e., clannishness] which is so offensive" (*Public Advertiser*, 2 May 1786). In the *Life*, Boswell would proudly reprint Courtenay's couplet and insert a footnote containing a new line that Courtenay had added to his third edition, published on 22 May 1786: "Scarce by *South* Britons now esteem'd a Scot" (Courtenay, 1786b, p. 25 n. 49; *Life*, 1:222–23 n. 1). Courtenay set off this line with a long quotation from the *Tour* that defended Johnson's anti-Scottish prejudice, in part because Johnson saw in Scots, as Boswell wrote, "that nationality which . . . no liberal-minded Scotchman will deny" (*Life*, 5:20). In the second edition of the *Life*, Johnson similarly imputes "the success of the Scotch in London . . . in a considerable degree to their spirit of nationality" (Boswell, 1793, 3:449; *Life*, 4:186). Boswell had broken most of his ties with Edinburgh and his old friends there, and his support network included none of its inhabitants except Sir William Forbes, who was firmly connected with Boswell's circle of friends in London. A refashioned identity as an assimilated Londoner helped Boswell both to bond with his friends there and to excuse Johnson's prejudice against his native land.

The London-centric character of Boswell's support network also reflected urban geography. Although at the end of the eighteenth century the population of greater London was roughly a million people spread over a large area, those Boswell needed to see for the *Life* were all accessible to him. He and the other members of "the Gang" lived close to one another in the western part of London, near the homes that Boswell rented successively at 56 Great Queen Street (from May 1786 to January 1789), 38 Queen Anne Street East (from January 1789 to January 1791), and 47 Great Portland Street (from January 1791). It was particularly fortunate that Malone lived just minutes away, on Queen Anne Street West, during the years when they were frequently collaborating on the *Life*. Courtenay also moved "within a few doors of me" at a critical time, as Boswell wrote in his journal on 21 February 1791. Boswell's principal contacts among booksellers and printers, like much of the book trade, were concentrated in the old City of London, from Fleet Street (Nichols), to New Bridge Street in Blackfriars (Baldwin, after moving from Fleet Street in 1789), to the Poultry (Dilly) farther east, with the largest concentration near the middle in Paternoster Row and St. Paul's Churchyard (Raven, 2014). From his various homes, these destinations were thirty or more minutes away on foot but quicker by hackney coach, and once in "the City" Boswell could walk without difficulty from one bookseller or printer to another. The printers of the main newspapers to which Boswell and his network kept up a steady stream of publicity and advertisements for the *Life* were also easily accessible within the City: Baldwin's *St. James's Chronicle*,

Woodfall's *Public Advertiser* in Paternoster Row, and the Strahans' *London Chronicle* in the Fleet Street neighborhood where Johnson had resided. Long before his move to London, Boswell recorded in his journal on 19 March 1772 that he was given his own room in the Dilly residence in the Poultry, with instructions to lodge there "whenever I was late in the City end of the town, . . . & consider it as my home."

2 Publishing the First Edition

After completing a draft of the *Life of Johnson*, Boswell wrote in his journal on 1 January 1790 that he "delivered the Introduction of it to Baldwin" – meaning the sheet of text that would eventually become the first seven pages in the first edition (*Life*, 1:25–34). He then admitted, however, that his action was a ruse, "that I might say my Book was *at* if not *in* the press on Newyear's day." Before the printing could begin in earnest, Boswell had to make several critical decisions in his capacity as the book's author-publisher. One of those decisions, that the book would be produced in the large and expensive quarto format, had already been made. The two writers whom Boswell considered his chief competition, Sir John Hawkins and Hester Lynch Piozzi, had recently published books about Johnson in the more modest octavo format (Piozzi, 1786; Hawkins, 1787), and Boswell wanted his biography of Johnson to have a higher status. But this plan was also a source of anxiety. On 15 October 1785 the *Morning Chronicle*, responding to the notice of the forthcoming "one Volume Quarto" appended to the *Tour* two weeks earlier, warned that "Boswell's octavo [i.e., *Tour*] bids fair to answer his purposes well; but let him beware of his vast design with which he threatens in a quarto. A *quartophobia* is, and ought to be, among the constitutional peculiarities of every man." Another issue – whether to publish in one quarto volume, as stated in the notice in the *Tour*, or two – was pondered but did not need to be determined with certainty until a later date. But three interrelated issues had to be resolved before the printing could begin: the size and quality of the paper, the size of the type, and the number of copies to be printed.

When publication was in its planning stages in January 1790, Baldwin wrote to Boswell about the first two of these matters. Boswell summarized Baldwin's letter (now lost) in his journal entry for Saturday 9 January 1790, when the book was still slated to be a one-volume quarto, large enough to cost one guinea (£1 1s.):

> I had been at Baldwin's before dinner, in consequence of a letter from him, which shewed me that by using a *pica* instead of an *english* letter in printing my Book, I might comprise it within such a number of sheets as a Guinea volume should contain, which I could not do in english letter unless upon

a *medium* instead of a *demy* paper, so as to have a larger page. I consulted with Dilly, and carried specimens of both kinds of paper to Baldwin's, where it was settled that I should on Monday have a specimen in each way.

On Monday the 11th Boswell accordingly went to Baldwin's and Dilly's, "consulting as to my Life of Johnson." His journal account continues: "From the computation of my manuscript or *Copy* as it is called there were 416000 words which we averaged would make too many pages in Quarto even upon *pica*, and therefore it was thought by Baldwin that I should make two Quarto volumes on *English* and sell them at 30 shillings." Baldwin, then, contemplated using either smaller (pica) or larger (English) type on either smaller (demy) or larger (medium) paper (Gaskell, 1995, pp. 73–74). But after calculating the length of the manuscript, he concluded that the work should be printed in two quarto volumes using English type and (presumably) demy paper. Baldwin believed that these two volumes would be of moderate thickness, as we know from his modest price estimate (for a two-volume quarto, that is) of thirty shillings.

It was at this point that Boswell recorded in his journal entry for 13 January 1790 that he "talked of printing my Life of Johnson in [a one-volume] Folio" (an unwieldy format used mainly for lectern books such as dictionaries) – until Malone told him that he "might as well throw it into the Thames, for a folio would not now be read." Malone had a different plan, as Boswell related:

> His scheme was to print 1000 on pica in Quarto, in one volume however thick, & at the same time by *over-running* the types as it is called to print 1000 in octavo, which would be kept in *petto* [i.e., in reserve] and be in readiness for sale, whenever the Quarto was sold. This scheme pleased me much & both Dilly & Baldwin approved of it; so I had resolved on it and got a specimen of each.

Malone's "scheme" for "*over-running* the types" was meant to keep costs down, thereby reducing risk, and to speed up the appearance of a second edition. A very thick one-volume quarto, printed with pica type, in a relatively small print run of 1,000 copies, would ensure a brisk sale of the first edition, after which a preprinted octavo second edition would be in readiness for quick release.

It was a good thing for Boswell that his support network was not limited to Malone, Baldwin, and Dilly. After sharing Malone's "scheme" with John Nichols, known for his knowledge of literary publishing, Boswell wrote in his journal entry for 13 January that Nichols "satisfied me it was a bad plan" for three reasons. "In the first place by *overrunning* I saved only £25 upon a hundred sheets, nothing being saved but the half of the Compositor's payment." Malone's plan would not do very much to reduce Boswell's publishing costs. "In the second place, my octavo edition would have all the errours of the Quarto." Boswell does not mention it, and we do not know if Nichols did either, but a crucial extension of this point is that besides being unable to correct errors, Boswell would have been unable to add new material and make other revisions and improvements if the second edition had been printed in advance.

Nichols's third reason was that a preprinted octavo second edition "would hurt the sale of my Quarto as its being ready would be known." It was common practice for expensive quarto first editions to be followed by cheaper octavo second editions, not unlike the way some books published as expensive hardbacks today appear later in less expensive paperback editions. But there were variations in this formula. Occasionally, as in the case of Adam Smith's *Wealth of Nations* (1776), a two-volume quarto first edition was more successful than anticipated, and the second edition was also issued in quarto (Sher, 2004, pp. 9–10), delaying publication of a more affordable octavo edition (until 1784, in Smith's case). Conversely, a quarto first edition might fall flat, with the result that a second edition would never appear. Nichols believed that as word leaked that an octavo second edition of the *Life* had been printed in advance, some potential buyers of the quarto edition would opt to wait for the cheaper octavo.

As an alternative to Malone's plan, Nichols "advised me rather to print 1500 in quarto, and assured me that I would run no risk of not disposing of that number." This advice must have injected Boswell with confidence at a critical time. Since he did not keep a fully written journal on a regular basis from about mid-January to May 1790, no other information has survived about the final decision-making process regarding these issues. But when printing began in late February or early March, Boswell had decided to print not 1,000 or even 1,500 but rather 1,750 copies, using pica type on medium paper, in hopes of confining the book to one very thick quarto volume costing one guinea. Dilly's impression account describes the paper as "fine Medium" and gives the price as twenty-two shillings per ream (Figure 6c), while Baldwin's account (Figure 7) identifies the print as "Pica, with Foot & Side Notes [i.e., footnotes at the bottom of the page and running side headers showing the date and Johnson's age, as in Figure 16b, upper left], on new Type." Baldwin's account dates the printing from April 1790 to May 1791, but that starting date must be incorrect, because on 12 March 1790 Boswell informed Percy that "a hundred pages are now printed," and on 9 April he told his friend Bennet Langton – a key informant about Johnson – that "I have printed twenty sheets [i.e., 160 pages] of my Magnum Opus. It will be the most entertaining Book that ever appeared" (Fifer, 1976, pp. 279, 289).

2.1 Turning Down *"A Cool thousand"*

Boswell's letter to Langton of 9 April 1790 that reported excitedly on the early printing of the *Life of Johnson* also contained another significant piece of news: "Only think of what an offer I have for it – *A Cool thousand*. But I am advised to retain the property myself." Who had offered him £1,000 for the copyright, and who had advised him to turn down that offer – and why? Boswell gave part of the answer three months later in a letter to Sir William Forbes of 2–3 July: Malone had told him of the offer from a bookseller whose identity Boswell did not yet know, and both Malone and Nichols had advised him against it on the grounds that his book (then still expected to be a one-volume quarto) would be likely to "clear £800 by the first edition, and it is thought better to take the chance of what subsequent profits may arrise, than to be content with a certain £200 more" (Sher, 2022, p. 188). Once again the support network had guided Boswell toward publication at his own risk. On 28 September 1790 Boswell boasted to his cousin and financial agent Robert Boswell: "I am a bold man to have refused *a cool thousand*. But my work may be called a view of literature and literary men in Great Britain for half a century" (quoted in Danziger & Brady, 1989, p. 110).

Meanwhile, the work kept getting longer, and consequently taking longer to complete, as Boswell added new text based on correspondence and conversations with those willing to help. As a result of this expansion, Boswell wrote in his journal on 8 September 1790, "my magnum opus must be in two volumes." On 11 October he proudly reported this information to Forbes, along with encouraging news about the progress of the printing: "My Life of Dr. Johnson has unavoidably swelled to two volumes, one of which is printed, and the other advancing rapidly," adding, "I would not now accept of £1500 for the property. Mr. Malone tells me I would get that but is clear I should refuse it. You cannot imagine what a rich and various treasure it will contain" (Sher, 2022, p. 208). As the book grew, so did the price. It would be neither the thirty-shilling, two-volume quarto envisioned by Baldwin earlier in the year nor a one guinea, one-volume quarto; rather, it would be two thick quarto volumes retailing for two guineas (42 shillings).

Throughout much of this period, Boswell was experiencing a phase of exalted spirits about his book, especially after he ended a demeaning relationship with an abusive political patron, Sir James Lowther, Earl of Lonsdale, in July 1790. He referred effusively to his "Magnum Opus" in his journal, in letters to friends, and in newspaper puffs, and he took bolder steps regarding publication. The choice of larger and more expensive paper, the expansion of the book into two expensive quarto volumes, the decision to print 1,750 copies, and the abrupt dismissal of a supposed opportunity to sell the copyright for £1,500 were all indications of his exhilarated state. But these decisions were made in consultation with members of his support group, and they would turn out to be wise choices from both a literary and a business standpoint. The same cannot be said, however, of his rash decision to purchase Knockroon – a parcel adjoining, and once part of, Auchinleck – when it came up for sale in the summer of 1790. Although already thousands of pounds in debt, and in the process of taking a huge risk on the *Life*, he committed himself to the purchase without seeking the advice of his banker and financial adviser Sir William Forbes or, as far as we know, anyone else.

The entire purchase price of Knockroon, £2,500, had to be raised through loans. In May 1790 one loan of £1,500 had been promised by his friend and Ayrshire neighbor Alexander Fairlie, who had first suggested that Boswell purchase Knockroon as far back as 1788 (Yale, C 1230 and 1233). That loan was enough for Boswell to secure the purchase in October 1790. When the time came to produce the remaining £1,000 early in the new year, however, Boswell grew fearful about publishing the *Life* at his own risk. In a letter of 18 January 1791 to Malone, then in Ireland, he confessed to being "so disturbed by sad money-matters that my mind has been quite fretful," and in this depressed state he admitted being "really tempted to accept of the £1000 for my Life of Johnson" (Baker, 1986, p. 389). Then, in what he termed "a most desponding and disagreable letter" to Malone on 29 January, he came clean about the full story of his "imprudent" purchase of Knockroon "at a time when I was sadly straitened," his "exceedingly embarrassed" financial circumstances, "the most woeful return of melancholy" for "some weeks," and his inclination to accept the offer of £1,000 if it was still available. But he was so uncertain – "quite at a loss what to do" – that he begged Malone to make the final determination: "Pray decide for me." He worried about having been told by George Steevens "that I have overprinted, and that the curiosity about Johnson is *now* only in our own circle" (Baker, 1986, pp. 393–95).

On 10 February 1791 Boswell told Malone that "my state of mind ... is harrassed by thinking of my debts. I am anxious to hear your determination as to my *Magnum Opus*" (Baker, 1986, p. 399). The situation grew so dire that on 20 February Boswell wrote in his journal that "Good Dilly allowed me to accept of the £1000 which I was now informed by a letter from Malone had been talked of for it by [the bookseller George] *Robinson*," and Dilly "in the most friendly manner pressed it, notwithstanding he should lose 7½ per cent agency [i.e., commission] on publication." But he also expressed reluctance to break from Dilly and remembered that "Malone had raised my hopes high of the success of my Work, & if it did succeed, the Quarto edition alone would yield me above

£1200." The next day Boswell calculated his finances for 1790, concluding that his annual "Debts" outweighed his annual "Funds" by £1,777 ("View of My Affairs," 21 February 1791, Yale, A 52). On 22 February Courtenay wrote to Malone in Ireland: "Poor Boswell is very low and dispirited and almost melancholy mad" (quoted in Danziger & Brady, 1989, p. 125). On 25 February Boswell informed Malone that he was "worse than you can possibly imagine" and "in a distressing perplexity how to decide as to the property of my Book," which he feared was now too big and too expensive, and was being denigrated by Steevens: "*Two Quartos* and *Two Guineas* sound in an alarming manner." This was "*quartophobia*" times two. In despair, Boswell returned to Robinson's offer:

> I believe in my present frame I should accept even of £500, for I suspect that were I now to talk to Robinson I should find him not disposed to give £1000. Did he absolutely *offer* it, or did he only express himself so as that you *concluded* he would give it? The pressing circumstance is that I *must* lay down £1000 by the first of May, on account of the purchase of land, which my old family enthusiasm urged me to make. (Baker, 1986, p. 405 & n. 7)

Replying on 5 March, Malone could not remember Robinson's exact words, "but the import, I think, was, that he was willing to give 1000£ for the copy." And since Robinson made his offer when he thought the work would be one volume, "I conceive he could not now offer for two less than 1200£" (Baker, 1986, p. 408).

Then the skies began to clear. In his next letter to Malone, on 9 March, Boswell described "a sudden relief from the inexplicable disorder which occasionally clouds my mind and makes me miserable." Flush with new loans of £200 each from Dilly and Baldwin, as well as £600 from an Ayrshire bank on the credit of rents from his estate, he no longer felt as desperate about the Knockroon purchase, and he declared himself "quite resolved now to keep the property of my Magnum Opus; and I flatter myself I shall not repent it" (Baker, 1986, pp. 410–13). Like any author risking both his literary reputation and a great deal of money on an ambitious publication, he continued to have "great anxiety about the sale of my Book," as he told Malone on 12 March. But when Courtenay, concerned about his friend's mental health, advised him to "accept of a thousand guineas" (£1,050) – if he could get that from Robinson (Baker, 1986, p. 415) – he held fast. Having made his final decision to publish at his own risk, he never again seriously doubted it in the two months before publication. By late March he was again enthusing in the newspapers about his "two stupendous *quartos*" (*Diary, or Woodfall's Register*, 28 March 1791).

The despondencies that tormented Boswell in the months preceding publication reveal him to have been financially stressed, psychologically troubled, and less than fully informed about the costs and realities of book publishing. From the time he delivered the "introduction" to his printer early in 1790 until late winter 1791, he fluctuated between thinking his book would be "a rich and various treasure" when his spirits were high to believing it was practically worthless when they were low, and between a confident refusal to accept as much as £1,500 for the copyright, if it were offered, and a willingness to accept as little as £500. That he even considered publishing in folio shows that he was out of step with the literary marketplace in the early 1790s. He did not understand that the copyright to a book of two thick quarto volumes was worth more than the same book in one volume. He consistently underestimated the time it would take to finish the *Life*. Left to his own devices, Boswell probably would not have possessed the mental stability, practical knowledge about publishing, and financial capacity necessary for making sound publishing decisions. His support network kept him safe and, for the most part, sane.

The loans from Dilly and Baldwin in the winter of 1791 show that the assistance Boswell's support network rendered was not limited to helpful advice and professional expertise. Baldwin's reply on 16 October 1787 to an earlier appeal by Boswell for a £200 loan is revealing: if necessary, he would be glad to provide it "at an hour's notice" (Yale, C 62). After receiving the Knockroon loan, Boswell thanked Dilly publicly in the opening lines of a poem titled "Ode to Mr. Charles Dilly," which Nichols published in the April 1791 issue of the *Gentleman's Magazine*: "My cordial Friend, / Still prompt to lend / Your cash when I have need on't;" (p. 367). Although Baldwin and Dilly stood to gain from Boswell's books, their generosity was grounded mainly in personal relationships, not financial self-interest. For both men, but especially Dilly, professional dealings with Boswell were part of a larger pattern of hospitality and friendship (Sher, 2006, p. 200). The same was true of Sir William Forbes, who in late January 1785 converted a large debt to his bank into an interest-only heritable bond, enabling Boswell to move his primary residence to London and produce the *Life of Johnson* there (Sher, 2022, p. lxxviii; Sher, forthcoming).

2.2 The Final Settlement

A year and a half after publication of the first edition of the *Life of Johnson*, Boswell received his reward. He described it in his journal entry for 24 November 1792 (Figure 5), written ten days later from his notes:

> This was the day fixed by Mr. Dilly for settling accounts with me and Mr. Baldwin as to the Quarto Edition of my Life of Dr. Johnson &c. I was somewhat animated by the prospect, and walked pretty briskly to my worthy Bookseller's where I had a hearty breakfast; after which he produced to me the clear produce of the sale exclusive of presents, amounting to £1555.18.2. This was very flattering to me as an Authour.

Figure 5 Boswell's journal entry for 24 November 1792, describing the first-edition settlement with Dilly and Baldwin. Beinecke Rare Book and Manuscript Library, Yale University, J 117, fols. 20–21

The party moved to Baldwin's, "where I cleared off a Bond for £400 (part of the price of Knockroon advanced to me by him & Mr. Dilly)" as well as a separate Baldwin loan for £100. "There was great satisfaction in thus paying principal & interest to two worthy friends who had assisted me with their credit." Boswell and Dilly then returned to Dilly's, "and after allowing for various sums which I owed him, there was a ballance due to me of £608." That afternoon Boswell "dined heartily at Baldwin's," where they were later joined by Dilly and Baldwin's sister and brother-in-law for an evening of whist and supper. It was a long day with his bookseller and his printer, whose shops were roughly fifteen minutes apart on foot, and at its end Boswell reported that he was "observed not to be in good spirits." But publication of the first edition of the *Life* was finally complete.

The journal passage just quoted captures the excitement and anticipation on the morning of the final settlement: Boswell is "animated by the prospect" of a profitable accounting; he walks "pretty briskly"; his bookseller is "worthy"; the breakfast is "hearty"; the profit of £1,555 18s. 2d. is "very flattering to me as an Authour." The upbeat mood continues, as he feels "great satisfaction" in paying back £500 in loans owed to Dilly and Baldwin, plus interest, and dines "heartily" at Baldwin's. But then he must pay back hundreds more to Dilly from previous loans. In the end, he is left with a little more than £600, or less than 40 percent of the profit he had found so "very flattering" in the morning. Although he does not mention it here, that £600 was owed to the Scottish bank from which he had borrowed the same sum for the purchase of Knockroon (he would pay it back two years later with interest; Baker, 1986, p. 410 n. 2). No wonder Boswell appears dejected at the conclusion of his journal entry.

Five days later Boswell wrote in his journal that he "gave a dinner, a kind of feast ... upon the success of my first edition of Dr. Johnson's Life," including toasts such as "Health and long life to the Life of Dr. Johnson." The guest list was limited to several individuals among Boswell's support network and some of their, and Boswell's own, family members: Malone; Nichols and his son-in-law Rev. John Pridden; Dilly and his brother "Squire [John] Dilly," who had entertained Boswell, Johnson, and Charles Dilly at his Bedfordshire estate in June 1781 (*Life*, 4:118–31); Baldwin and his teenage son Charles (Griffiths, 2004), who was in the process of succeeding his father as the printer of the *Life*; Boswell's brother David, daughters Veronica and Euphemia, and son James; and Isaac Reed. The way Boswell describes his state of mind at this event is much like his account of the final settlement: "I got into a pretty good state of joviality, though still dreary at bottom."

Why was Isaac Reed at Boswell's celebratory "feast"? Reed was a close friend of Malone, Dilly, and Nichols, and Boswell's journal and correspondence record many of their dinners at which both Boswell and Reed were present in the three years leading up to publication of the *Life*. Boswell was indebted to "steady Reed" for help with the chronology of Johnson's life and for providing a list of notes and corrections for the second edition, where he would receive praise for assisting Johnson with his biographical prefaces on the English poets (Boswell, 1793, 3:281–82; *Life*, 4:37; Baker, 1986, p. 360; Sherbo, 1989, pp. 112–13; Waingrow, 2001, pp. 247–48, 382–87). Equally important, Reed provided an opportunity for Boswell to publish an anonymous autobiographical account in the May and June 1791 issues of the *European Magazine*, "Memoirs of James Boswell, Esq." (reproduced in Pottle, 1929, pp. xxix–xliv). Boswell used this opportunity to promote himself and his publications, including a gloating reference to "his great literary work in which he was engaged for many years, '*The Life of Dr. Johnson*,' which he has at last published, in two volumes quarto, and which has been received by the world with extraordinary approbation." This puff is followed by a sentence added by the editor: "In our next and subsequent Numbers we shall give a review of this very instructive and entertaining piece of biography." The anonymous favorable review of the *Life* in the *European Magazine* – possibly by Reed himself – began appearing in the August (rather than July) 1791 issue (20:107) and extended through ten installments, reaching its climax a few weeks before the final settlement with Dilly and Baldwin with a reference to "the faithful Biographer" and "his excellent, instructive, and entertaining work" (October 1792, 21:286). Boswell, then, had good reasons to invite Reed to his celebratory dinner, and his doing so reminds us how much the success of the *Life of Johnson* owed to the long tentacles of Boswell's support network in the press.

The dismal state of his finances is probably the principal reason Boswell wavered between elation and depression after the settlement of the first edition. Owing to his debts and his "imprudent" purchase of Knockroon, he would get little pleasure beyond pride from the monetary rewards obtained from the *Life*. If he had not purchased Knockroon, he told Forbes on 27 September 1791, he had intended to apply his book profits to his debt to Forbes's bank (Sher, 2022, p. 226). The only questions were which debts he was going to pay down or pay off with his profits from the *Life*, and by how much.

Our primary concern, however, is not with what Boswell did with his publishing profits but with how he acquired them. We begin that inquiry by asking a fundamental question: how did Dilly arrive at the "very flattering" sum of £1,555 18s. 2d.?

3 Accounting for the First Edition

3.1 Copies, Commission, Expenses, Profit

Figure 6 reproduces Dilly's impression account for the first edition. It begins with a list of the recipients of the 61 sets that were not intended for sale (6a & 6b). Nine of those sets would be sent in sheets (i.e., unbound) to Stationers' Hall. The remaining 52 sets were claimed by Boswell himself. Most were put in boards and delivered by Dilly as presentation copies, presumably with inscriptions written by Boswell, several of which have been traced to their current locations (Seymour, 2016, pp. 420–24). Dilly's list includes 13 sets earmarked for "The Authour," 11 in boards and 2 in sheets. On a separate page titled "Delivered to Myself 13" (Yale, A 59 (3)), Boswell identified most of the people who were to receive those 13 copies, including "My two sons" – Alexander and James (whose inscribed copy has been traced by Terry Seymour) – "My brother T.D.," and "Mr. [John] Taylor," a newspaper editor who had earned his presentation copy by persuading Boswell to change the word "*Containing*" to "*Comprehending*" in the title of the book (Taylor, 1832, 1:109–10).

Many of the presentation copies went to members of Boswell's support network, including Baldwin, Malone, Nichols, Tomlins, Langton, Courtenay, Forbes, and Reynolds. The three copies given to Tomlins may have constituted payment for his indexing services (Seymour, 2016, pp. 422–23), or perhaps Tomlins was the conduit for gift copies intended for two others in Baldwin's shop: the principal compositor, John Plymsell, and the principal corrector, "Mr. Selfe." In addition to the personal copy for Nichols, a copy marked "John Nichols for the Magazine" meant the *Gentleman's Magazine*, which would print an enthusiastic blurb in its May 1791 issue (61:466–67) before continuing its positive notice in subsequent issues. The June issue also contained a long letter from Nichols that concluded: "no book that has appeared in this age deserves better the popularity which it has already obtained, and which will undoubtedly increase" (61:500; Hart, 1952, p. 402). The list of recipients includes William Johnson Temple, to whom Boswell confided regularly about his progress, and other friends and acquaintances who had contributed to the book, such as Sir William Scott, John Philip Kemble, Capel Lofft, John Wilkes, John Douglas, then Bishop of Carlisle (who would join The Club in 1792), and Boswell's informant about Jacobite issues, Andrew Lumisden. Presentation copies also went to several of Johnson's friends who had provided Boswell with information about his subject, such as Edmund Hector, Warren Hastings, and William Seward, and to individuals to whom Boswell owed other kinds of debts, such as Alexander Fairlie, who had loaned him money and advised him about estate management; Henry Sampson Woodfall, whose *Public Advertiser* was, like Baldwin's *St. James's Chronicle*, a reliable outlet for Boswellian chatter (e.g., Yale, P 100.1 (2–7); Pottle, 1971, pp. 1224–33); his exiled Corsican friend Pasquale Paoli, who had lavished hospitality on him in London for many years; and the engraver of the frontispiece portrait, James Heath.

Oddly, one of the central figures in Boswell's publishing network, Charles Dilly, is not on the list of those receiving presentation copies, though the list

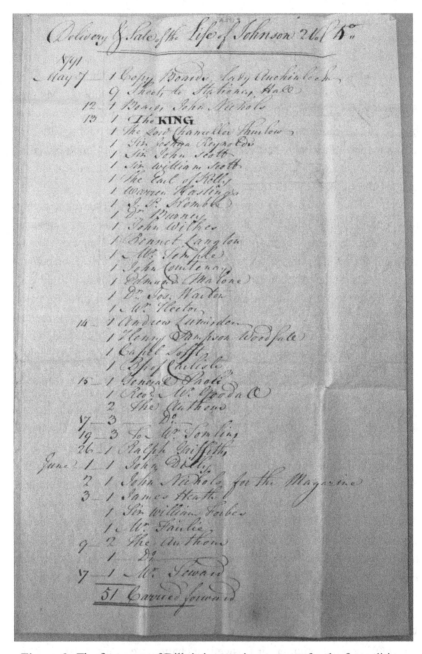

Figure 6a The first page of Dilly's impression account for the first edition, showing 51 of the 61 copies removed from sale. Beinecke Rare Book and Manuscript Library, Yale University, A 59 (4 & 5)

The second page of Dilly's impression account (Figure 6b) subtracts the 61 copies designated for Stationers' Hall (9) and for Boswell's personal and presentation copies (52) from the total number of sets printed, 1,750, to arrive at the number of copies for sale: 1,689. It then multiplies that number by the wholesale price of £1 12s. (32 shillings) per set to reach the sum of £2,702 8s. This was the gross publishing income from the edition. When Dilly sold a set of the *Life* to a customer for the retail price of 2 guineas in boards, he was entitled, like any other retail bookseller, to 10 shillings profit, minus the cost of boarding each set. But the publisher received 32 shillings for each set sold, and therefore the £2,702 8s. generated by sales at the wholesale price belonged entirely to Boswell.

The second page of the impression account concludes with a category headed "Dr.," meaning "Debtor," or the charges that Boswell owed to Dilly. There are two such items. First, "To Expences of the Impression as p[e]r. Account Opposite" refers to the total of all the charges for printing, paper, engraving, advertising, and various incidentals, as listed on the next page of the statement (Figure 6c). This immense sum, £943 16s. 4d., is analyzed in Section 3.2. The second item listed by Dilly in the "Dr." category is "Commission 7½ p[er]cent," meaning the payment Dilly received for managing all aspects of the publication. To calculate it, Dilly took 7½ percent of the gross receipts from the trade sale (£2,702 8s.). The product of this calculation, £202 13s. 6d., was not an insignificant amount of money, but it was a fraction of the publishing profit generated by Boswell's book.

Although the impression account does not show the final totals, Dilly computed them on a separate scrap of paper (Yale, A 59 (4 & 5)). Subtracting £1,146 9s. 10d. (Boswell's total expenses, combining charges of £943 16s. 4d. with Dilly's commission of £202 13s. 6d.) from £2,702 8s. (the gross wholesale income), he arrived at £1,555 18s. 2d. – precisely the amount Boswell had found so "very flattering to me as an Authour" at the account settlement.

3.2 "A Monstrous List of Expences and Deductions"

The third page of Dilly's impression account (Figure 6c) reveals how Dilly arrived at £943 16s. 4d. as the total charges Boswell owed for publishing the first edition. In 1775, when James Beattie was asked by a friend how to go about arranging his first publication, Beattie advised him to sell the copyright to a bookseller for a fixed amount and to avoid conditional arrangements, for "You cannot imagine what a monstrous list of expences and deductions a Bookseller draws forth in array against an author, when they come to settle

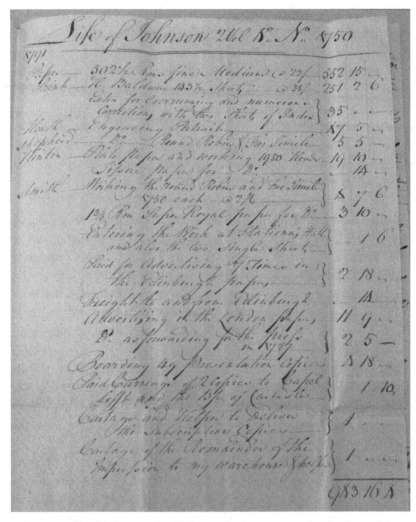

Figure 6c The third page of Dilly's impression account for the first edition, itemizing Boswell's charges. Beinecke Rare Book and Manuscript Library, Yale University, A 59 (4 & 5)

their accounts upon an agreement of that sort" (quoted in Sher, 2006, p. 214). Unlike Beattie, who was averse to risk and suspicious of booksellers, Boswell would not have doubted the integrity of his good friend Dilly when confronted with the lengthy list of "expences and deductions" for which he was responsible.

3.2.1 Paper and Print

Approximately 89 percent of the charges that Dilly passed along to Boswell came from two components: paper and print. They were nowhere near equal: the paper charge, in round numbers, of £553 (for 502½ reams of "fine Medium" paper at 22s. per ream, yielding 251,750 sheets at 500 sheets per ream) was almost twice the £286 charge for standard and "Extra" printing. Paper cost significantly more than printing in eighteenth-century books because it was made from waste linen, a manufactured product in short supply; the age of cheap paper made from wood pulp with steam-driven machines would not arrive until the second half of the nineteenth century. But in this case the imbalance was even more than usual because so many sheets of expensive "fine Medium" paper were required for a quarto edition with a large print run. Besides the high cost of the paper, there was also the matter of supply: on one occasion in late 1790, Boswell told Malone that printing was delayed because of "an unaccountable neglect in having paper enough in readiness" (Baker, 1986, p. 382).

According to Baldwin's printing statement (Figure 7), the printer used 143½ sheets of paper per two-volume set (yielding 1,150 quarto pages), including 1¾ sheets for "Cancels" (corrected pages added after the book was printed). This large quantity of paper was required because the first edition of the *Life* consisted of 1,104 numbered pages of text (516 in volume one and 588 in volume two), in addition to the title page and 25 pages of front matter in volume one (a 5-page dedication to Reynolds, a 4-page Advertisement, a 15-page

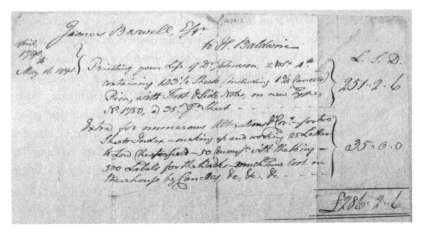

Figure 7 "Mr. Baldwin's Account for printing my Life of Dr. Johnson" (as endorsed by Boswell). Beinecke Rare Book and Manuscript Library, Yale University, A 59 (2)

Alphabetical Table of Contents, and a page of Corrections and Additions) and the title page in volume two. Taking into consideration the equipment (including type) and labor used in the printing process, and the size of the print run, Baldwin set the cost of printing at 35 shillings per sheet. He arrived at the base cost for printing the book (£251 2s. 6d.) by multiplying this printing rate per sheet by the total number of sheets of paper used per set (143½).

Boswell certainly got his money's worth from Baldwin's shop (Redford, 2002, ch. 1). The manuscript copy arrived intermittently over a long period of time – beginning in January 1790 and not ending until just before publication in mid-May 1791. It was often heavily, and messily, revised, with many cross-outs and insertions between the lines and in the margins. In addition to the manuscript, there were hundreds of "Papers Apart" that had to be inserted correctly. The task of typesetting this textual clutter fell mainly to Plymsell and, if necessary, Selfe, who had proved himself capable of deciphering the most challenging parts of Boswell's manuscript of the *Tour* (Baker, 1986, p. 268). The editors of the manuscript edition of the *Life* have discovered some instances in which handwriting was misread, directions misunderstood, or words and even one whole passage overlooked. Yet the overall impression is of "recognition for the compositors' routinely heroic feats of typesetting which, despite some important lapses, produced surprisingly few misreadings of Boswell's often tortuous copy" (Bonnell, 2012, p. xviii).

This assessment is consistent with the testimony of Boswell and Malone. While the first volume was being printed, and Boswell was dreading being called away by Lonsdale on political business, he wrote in his journal on 14 June 1790 that he "breakfasted with honest Baldwin my Printer" and arranged for "my compositor Plymsell an intelligent and accurate man" to "have other employment that he might leave, and resume my Book on my return." When Boswell went to Carlisle with Lonsdale three days later, Malone continued working on the book with Plymsell and reported on 8 July that "Your compositor has gone on very smartly" (Baker, 1986, p. 373). The high quality of Plymsell's work was probably the reason Boswell decided in January 1791 to "have but one compositor" after a period of using two or more (Baker, 1986, p. 395). Nor was Plymsell's role limited to accurate typesetting. At times Plymsell questioned the text and even altered it, as when he changed a reference to James Macpherson from "a man better known in both countries" to "another Scotchman, who has found means to make himself well known both in Scotland and England" (Redford & Goldring 1998, pp. 130, 259). Similarly, Selfe regularly questioned, and sometimes altered, Boswell's spelling, punctuation, diction, and even content (see the many entries under "Plymsell" and "Selfe" in the indexes to Bonnell, 2012 & 2019). In the Advertisement to the second edition, Boswell paid tribute to the typographical excellence of Baldwin's shop (Boswell, 1793, 1:xiii–xiv; *Life*, 1:10).

Plymsell and Selfe, then, were vital parts of Boswell's support network. There are also indications that Boswell himself was deeply involved in overseeing the printing process. His journal entry for 20 April 1790 records a breakfast with Plymsell, and it is likely that other meetings of this kind went unrecorded because the journal was often sparse or totally neglected when the *Life* was being put through the press. Nevertheless, on multiple occasions the journal records visits to Baldwin's shop (e.g., on 2 February 1790, "Printing House to quicken [the printing]"; on 2 February 1791, "went to the Printinghouse"; on 5 February, "was twice at the printing house"). When Boswell left for Carlisle with Lonsdale on 17 June 1790, he remarked in his journal that "It vexed me that I was dragged away from the printing of my Life of Johnson." A week after his return to London, his journal entry for 24 July reveals that he "Went to Baldwin's Printing office where I was happy to find myself again, though I found neither my friend Baldwin the master, Selfe the Corrector, nor Plymsell the Compositor." The manuscript of the *Life* contains many notes and instructions that Boswell addressed to Plymsell and Selfe, often by name, and we may presume that some of these matters were resolved on site. Thus, printing the *Life of Johnson* resembled a fourteen-month negotiation among Boswell, Malone, Plymsell, and Selfe, with a fluid interplay of activity, both in writing and in person. It was, in short, an example of what Jerome McGann has called "a continual collaborative process" (quoted in Redford, 2002, p. 48).

Of particular interest in Dilly's and Baldwin's accounts is the £35 that Baldwin charged for various extras. Dilly summarized these additional charges in his account as "Extra for Overrunning and numerous Correction, with two sheets of Index." Baldwin provided more detail: "Extra for numerous Alterations & Cor[rection]s. – for two Sheets Index – making up and working 25 Letter to Lord Chesterfield – 50 Convers[atio]n. with the King – 500 Labels for the Backs – much Time lost in Warehouse by Cancles [*sic*], &c, &c, &c." Baldwin's phrase "numerous Alterations and Cor[rection]s" refers to changes to the manuscript after it had been submitted, changes to the printed proof sheets before the type was redistributed, and changes to the corrected proof sheets (the "revises"), and second revises that were sometimes insisted on by Boswell (Powell, 1928, p. 54). The indexes to the four volumes of the manuscript edition of the *Life*, especially the third and fourth volumes (Bonnell, 2012 & 2019), list so many of these kinds of changes that it seems doubtful that Baldwin charged Boswell fully for the labor of Plymsell, Selfe, Tomlins, and others in his shop who worked on the book so diligently for so long.

The alterations and corrections Baldwin charged to Boswell also included the labor required for cancels, which were the most expensive variety of changes because they occurred after the printing was finished and the type redistributed. Given the length and complexity of the *Life*, it is remarkable that it contains so few cancels. Pottle lists them and explains why each occurred (Pottle, 1929, pp. 150–55). Most of the five cancels in volume two were insisted on by individuals who wanted their names removed (Redford, 2002, pp. 43–47), and in two instances of this kind Boswell was reimbursed for the expense of the cancels by the protesting party, William Gerard Hamilton (Boswell, 1791b, 2:353–54, 395–96). The most significant cancel (Figure 8) tempered Johnson's approving remarks on male conjugal infidelity (Boswell, 1791b, 2:301–2; *Life*,

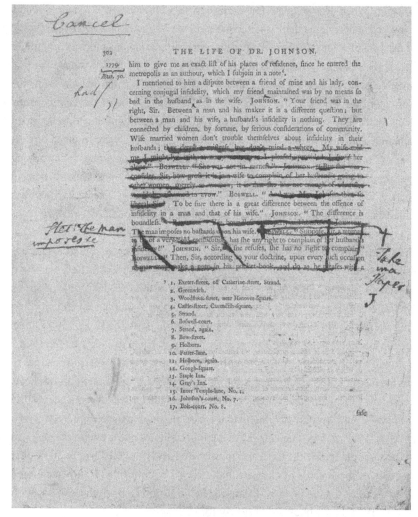

Figure 8 Canceled passage containing Johnson's views on conjugal infidelity in the quarto first edition (2:302). Houghton Library, Harvard University, MS Hyde 51 (23)

3:406), which Boswell commented on in his letter to Malone of 10 February 1791: "I wonder how you and I admitted this to the publick eye" (Baker, 1986, pp. 400–1).

Another extra printing expense, marked "two Sheets Index" in Baldwin's list of charges, was the addition of an "Alphabetical Table of Contents, To Both Volumes" (Figure 9). This came about in late January 1791, when it became clear that the second volume was going to be considerably longer than the first.

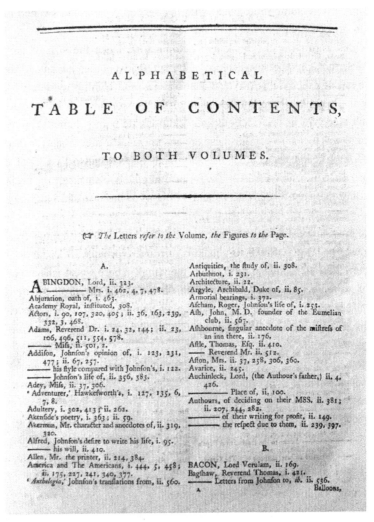

Figure 9 The first page of Thomas Tomlins's Alphabetical Table of Contents, prefixed to the first volume of the first edition to provide an index and to help to balance the lengths of the two volumes. Beinecke Rare Book and Manuscript Library, Yale University

In his letter to Malone of 29 January, Boswell remarked that "The *Counsellor* [Tomlins] indeed has devised an ingenious way to thicken the first volume, by *prefixing* the Index" (Baker, 1986, p. 395). Most of the work was complete by 14 February, when Boswell wrote in his journal that he "drank tea by appointment with the Corrector of his [i.e., Baldwin's] press, Mr. Tomlins who ... shewed me a good part of an Index to my Life of Johnson, which he had offered to make, and offering to do it very reasonably had been desired by me to go on with it." He added that he "intended to *prefix* it as an *Alphabetical Table of Contents* to make my first volume more equal with my second, which had swelled much beyond my computation."

Besides improving the book and helping to balance the size of the two volumes, the Alphabetical Table of Contents had another advantage. Since two sheets of paper yielded sixteen quarto pages, and Tomlins used only fifteen of them, Boswell gained another page of front matter, which he used for an unnumbered page of "Corrections and Additions" to both volumes (Figure 10). Yet there was a cost to pay for these enhancements. Besides whatever Boswell paid Tomlins, and the cost of the additional paper, Baldwin's £35 of extra charges must have included £3 10s. for printing the two sheets of the prefatory index and the page of corrections and additions at the rate of 35 shillings per sheet.

The most interesting extra printing charge is termed "overrunning" by Dilly and described by Baldwin as "making up and working 25 Letter to Lord Chesterfield – 50 Convers[atio]n. with the King." These references are to two quarto pamphlets excerpted from the *Life*, one titled *The Celebrated Letter from Samuel Johnson, LL.D. to Philip Dormer Stanhope, Earl of Chesterfield* (Figure 11) and the other *A Conversation between His Most Sacred Majesty George III. and Samuel Johnson* (Boswell, 1790a; 1790b). The *Letter to Chesterfield*, a mere two pages of text, contains the indignant letter that Johnson composed in February 1755, mocking the earl's empty promise to be his patron. The six-page *Conversation* consists of Boswell's account of Johnson's interview with George III in February 1767. The title pages of both pamphlets show Baldwin as the printer and Dilly as the publisher, 1790 as the date, and "Half a Guinea" (10s. 6d.) as the absurdly high price, and both pamphlets announce on the next page "Entered in the Hall-Book of the Company of Stationers."

These pamphlets were never intended for publication and were never put into circulation. Rather, they were part of a publicity stunt orchestrated by Boswell. By printing these pamphlets, registering them at Stationers' Hall on 29 April 1791, promoting them in newspaper advertisements that drew attention to their being "separately entered in Stationer's Hall" (*Public Advertiser*, 30 April

CORRECTIONS AND ADDITIONS,

Which the Reader is requested to make with his Pen, before perusing the following Life.

VOLUME I.

P. 32, l. 3 from the foot, *for* cotemporaries, *read* contemporaries.

P. 80, l. 13, *dele* out.

Page 133, line 24, *for* a warren, *read* free warren.

P. 136, l. 6, *for* is certainly the performance of Dr. Charles Bathurst, *read* has been erroneously ascribed to Dr. Bathurst, whose christian name was Richard.

P. 173, l. 16, 17, 24, 26, *for* Jennings, *read* Jennyns.

P. 160, l. 8, *for* Pancoek, *read* Panckoucke.

P. 195, l. 4, *upon the word* name *put the following note* :—I have had inquiry made in Ireland as to this story, but do not find it recollected there. I give it on the authority of Dr. Johnson, to which may be added, that of " The Biographical Dictionary," in which it has stood many years.

Ibid. l. 4, *for* a book on the authenticity of the Gospel History, *read* " An Enquiry into the Origin of Moral Virtue."

Ibid. l. 13 & 14, *for* Innys *read* Innes.

P. 303, *for* Νὺξ ιεχετωι, *read* Νὺξ γαϱ ιεχετωι.

P. 329, l. 25, *for* drives *read* drove.

P. 344, l. 18, *for* wrote, *read* written.

P. 374, l. 24, *for* been a witness against, *read* connected with.

VOLUME II.

P. 191, l. 8, *for* Johnston *read* Johnson.

P. 346, l. 12, *for* one of his excellent prefatory discourses to his plays, *read* his excellent Dedication of his Juvenal.

Ibid. l. 15, *after* novelty *insert* and.

P. 367, in Note, *for* Chalmers, *read* Chambers.

P. 352, l. 16, *after* Pope *insert* inverted commas, *and* dele *them* l. 17, *after* imposition.

Ibid. after him *put a comma.*

P. 381, l. 22, *dele* in.

P. 397, in the note, for *communis illa*, read *communis in illa.*

P. 458, before the letter to the Reverend Dr. Taylor, *insert,*

To Mr. EDMUND ALLEN.

" DEAR SIR,

" IT has pleased GOD this morning to deprive me of the powers of speech; and as I do not know but that it may be his farther good pleasure to deprive me soon of my senses, I request you will, on the receipt of this note, come to me, and act for me, as the exigencies of my case may require. I am sincerely yours,

" SAM. JOHNSON."

P. 562, l. 3, from the foot, after *tongue* insert a ——, and prefix inverted commas to the following word.

P. 582, l. 10, *after* respectable contribution, *add*—But the Dean and Chapter of St. Paul's having come to a resolution of admitting monuments there, upon a liberal and magnificent plan, that cathedral was afterwards fixed on as the place.

THE

Figure 10 This page of Corrections and Additions was prefixed to the first volume of the first edition, on the last page of the two sheets containing the Alphabetical Table of Contents. Beinecke Rare Book and Manuscript Library, Yale University

1791, in Tankard, 2014, pp. 260–61), announcing their (bogus) publication date as 12 May 1791 (four days before publication of the *Life*), and boasting about his actions in a newspaper article on 17 May (Tankard, 2014, p. 265), Boswell put himself in a position to demand an apology from newspapers and magazines that excerpted these pamphlets (as he probably hoped they would), because they were legally his property. He produced a mock, self-serving apology in the *London Packet* for that purpose, in which the offending periodical states that it is sorry for

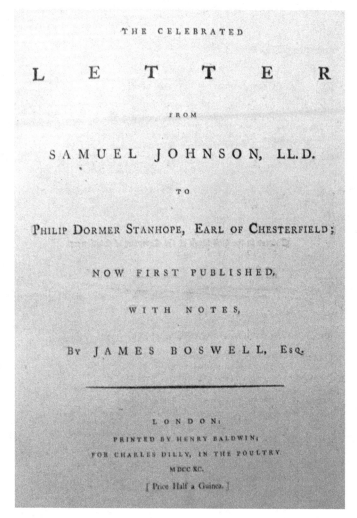

THE CELEBRATED

L E T T E R

FROM

SAMUEL JOHNSON, LL.D.

TO

PHILIP DORMER STANHOPE, EARL OF CHESTERFIELD;

NOW FIRST PUBLISHED,

WITH NOTES,

BY JAMES BOSWELL, ESQ.

LONDON:
PRINTED BY HENRY BALDWIN;
FOR CHARLES DILLY, IN THE POULTRY.
M DCC XC.
[Price Half a Guinea.]

Figure 11 Twenty-five copies of the *Letter to Chesterfield* were run off while the first volume of the *Life of Johnson* was being printed during late winter or early spring 1790. Beinecke Rare Book and Manuscript Library, Yale University

printing these two works, "but Mr. Boswell is too candid to take any advantage, and upon our assuring him of the fact, he declared he will not prosecute." It is highly suspicious that the manuscript of this apology (now in the Houghton Library, Harvard University, MS Eng 1386 (16)) was formerly owned by Nichols (Pottle, 1929, 138; Pooley, 2011, pp. 169, 172), and that Nichols's friend Alexander Chalmers, who was affiliated with the *Gentleman's Magazine*, *London Packet*, *St. James's Chronicle*, and other newspapers and periodicals, disclosed that Boswell wrote this mock apology in Dilly's shop (Nichols &

Nichols, 1817–58, 7:344). It is equally suspicious that the *London Packet* printed both an excerpt from the pamphlets and Boswell's mock apology on 21 May (Brown, 1991, p. 11) – the same day that the *St. James's Chronicle* (printed by Baldwin and edited by Tomlins) reprinted the apology from the *London Packet* (also printed by Baldwin) under the heading "Literary Property," with additional commentary by Boswell that calls it "a fair specimen of confidence, and that liberality which shou'd subsist between the different votaries of Literature" (Figure 12; Tankard, 2014, pp. 268–69; Yale, P 100.1 (7)). From all this it is evident that Boswell's intention was not to prevent newspapers or other biographers from reprinting this material, or to set a "trap" for them, as others have suggested (Pottle, 1929, pp. 134–41, quoting p. 141; Horne, 1950; Fleeman,

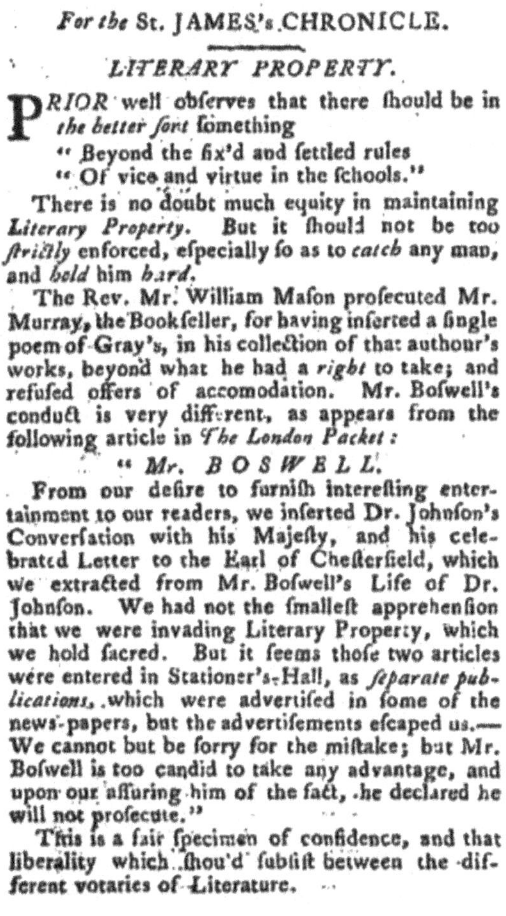

For the St. JAMES's CHRONICLE.

LITERARY PROPERTY.

PRIOR well obferves that there fhould be in *the better fort* fomething
" Beyond the fix'd and fettled rules
" Of vice and virtue in the fchools."

There is no doubt much equity in maintaining *Literary Property.* But it fhould not be too *ftrictly* enforced, efpecially fo as to *catch* any man, and *hold* him *hard.*

The Rev. Mr. William Mafon profecuted Mr. Murray, the Bookfeller, for having inferted a fingle poem of Gray's, in his collection of that author's works, beyond what he had a *right* to take; and refufed offers of accomodation. Mr. Bofwell's conduct is very different, as appears from the following article in *The London Packet:*

" *Mr. BOSWELL.*
From our defire to furnifh interefting entertainment to our readers, we inferted Dr. Johnfon's Converfation with his Majefty, and his celebrated Letter to the Earl of Chefterfield, which we extracted from Mr. Bofwell's Life of Dr. Johnfon. We had not the fmalleft apprehenfion that we were invading Literary Property, which we hold facred. But it feems thofe two articles were entered in Stationer's-Hall, as *feparate publications,* which were advertifed in fome of the news-papers, but the advertifements efcaped us.— We cannot but be forry for the miftake; but Mr. Bofwell is too candid to take any advantage, and upon our affuring him of the fact, he declared he will not profecute."

This is a fair fpecimen of confidence, and that liberality which fhou'd fubfift between the different votaries of Literature.

Figure 12 This article in the *St. James's Chronicle*, 21 May 1791, was part of an elaborate publicity stunt staged by Boswell and some of his associates. Burney Newspapers Collection

2000, p. 1727). Rather, Boswell intended to fabricate an incident that would generate publicity for the *Life* and at the same time enable himself to appear magnanimous, and Dilly, Baldwin, Tomlins, Nichols, Woodfall, and Chalmers – as well as Malone (Baker, 1986, p. 418) – were all in on the scheme.

Chalmers later remarked that Boswell's mock apology inspired him to write his humorous parody of the *Life of Johnson*, "Lesson in Biography; or, How to Write the Life of One's Friend" (originally published in the *Public Advertiser* and other newspapers in early July 1791; reprinted in Werkmeister, 1963, pp. 32–36). In this satire, a Dr. Pozz pontificates ridiculously in Johnson's characteristically contrarian style, as recorded by James Bozz. When Bozz is away from the doctor "for six weeks, three days, and seven hours, as I find by a memorandum in my journal," Dr. Pozz sends him a brief letter that begins "My bowels have been very bad." "It would have been unpardonable to have omitted a letter like this," Bozz remarks, "in which we see so much of his great and illuminated mind." Although "Lesson in Biography" has been viewed as "More damaging" (Danziger & Brady, 1989, p. 146) and "more devastating" (Werkmeister, 1963, p. 32) than various hostile reviews of the *Life*, Boswell did not see it that way. Chalmers commented that Boswell "often took an opportunity in my company to praise it" and intended to include it in the second edition of the *Life* until "dissuaded" from doing so (Nichols & Nichols, 1817–58, 7:344; Yale, P 100 (37), P 101 (4)). For Boswell, who reacted forcefully to criticism he considered scurrilous, Chalmers's parody, like his own mock apology, was good fun and, equally important, good publicity.

Baldwin records printing 25 copies of the *Letter to Chesterfield* and 50 copies of the *Conversation*, leaving just 16 and 41 copies, respectively, after 9 copies of each work were sent to Stationers' Hall – further evidence that these pamphlets were never intended for sale. The decision to print twice as many copies of the *Conversation* must have occurred late in the printing process, as Boswell initially planned to have an equal number of the two pamphlets "thrown off" (Chapman, 1928, p. 26). Although it is not known what Boswell did with these pamphlets, it is quite possible that he distributed them to newspapers and magazines as part of his scheme. They were printed from the same type as the *Life*, but with embellishments to create the impression of separate printing (Pottle, 1929, p. 136). We know approximately when they were printed – the *Letter to Chesterfield* in late winter or early spring 1790 and the *Conversation* later that spring – because that was when the printing of those parts of the first volume of the *Life* occurred (Pottle, 1929, p. 137). This circumstance accounts for the date 1790 appearing in the imprints, though the feigned date of publication was 12 May 1791. These two pamphlets must have accounted for a considerable portion of Baldwin's £35 charge for "extra" printing.

Baldwin's list of extra printing charges also includes "500 Labels for the Backs," meaning the labels for 250 two-volume sets in boards (Figure 4). It is not known why Boswell chose to print this quantity of labels, which far exceeded the number needed for his presentation copies. Finally, when Baldwin registers "much Time lost in Warehouse by Cancles [*sic*], &c, &c, &c.," the closing string of "&c's" masks various other extra printing jobs that Baldwin chose not to specify.

3.2.2 Engravings

The next six charges in Dilly's impression account concern the three engravings that Boswell commissioned for the *Life of Johnson*. One of those engravings – consisting of facsimiles of Johnson's handwriting at the ages of sixteen, thirty-five, and seventy-five – is of minor significance for the book, and its placement after the last page of text in volume two is anticlimactic. The other two engravings made important contributions, however, and both were shaped by members of Boswell's support network. The first encountered by readers is the engraved portrait of Johnson that serves as the frontispiece in volume one (Figure 1a), listed in the impression account as "Heath – Engraving Portrait – [£]47 5[s]." James Heath (Figure 13) was then making a name for himself as one of London's foremost engravers for the book trade. In 1785 he had done a line engraving of Samuel Johnson, after a painting by John Opie, for the frontispiece of James Harrison's one-volume folio edition of Johnson's *Dictionary of the English Language* (Figure 14; Johnson, 1786; Clingham, 2017, pp. 75–77). On 16 November 1785, after this work had begun appearing in parts that would be gathered into a volume in 1786, Harrison promoted Heath's performance in the *Times* as "a Large Magnificent Ornamental PORTRAIT of Dr. JOHNSON, from an Original Painting by OPIE, Engraved by HEATH, and alone worth at least HALF-A-GUINEA [10s. 6d.]."

Boswell must have seen and admired Heath's engraving of Johnson from Opie's portrait, which is cited in a footnote in the *Life* listing painted and engraved likenesses of Johnson (*Life*, 4:421 n. 2). For the frontispiece in his book, however, an engraving made from a portrait by Sir Joshua Reynolds was preferable. Since Reynolds was careful about who was allowed to engrave his paintings, and in 1789 had authorized Heath to make a stipple engraving from his 1779 portrait of George III, he may have recruited Heath for the frontispiece of the *Life*. Boswell was particularly attracted to the first portrait of Johnson that Reynolds had painted (though not completed) in 1756–7 (Mannings, 2000, text vol., p. 280), showing him as a thoughtful man of letters, seated in his study with quill and paper. In the *Life*, Boswell states that at the time of his first meeting with Johnson on 16 May 1763,

MR *HEATH*,
Historical Engraver to the King.

Published for the Proprietors of the Monthly Mirror, by T.Bellamy, King St.Covent Garden, June 1796.

Figure 13 The May 1796 issue of the *Monthly Mirror* published this print of James Heath, "Historical Engraver to the King," along with a brief profile of his career. Heath-Caldwell Family Archive

I had a very perfect idea of Johnson's figure, from the portrait of him painted by Sir Joshua Reynolds soon after he had published his Dictionary, in the attitude of sitting in his easy chair in deep meditation, which was the first picture his friend did for him, which Sir Joshua very kindly presented to me, and from which an engraving has been made for this work. (*Life*, 1:392)

Figure 14 Detail from James Heath's frontispiece engraving of Samuel Johnson, from a portrait by John Opie, in James Harrison's folio edition of Johnson's *Dictionary* (1786). Beinecke Rare Book and Manuscript Library, Yale University

In an earlier draft, Boswell indicated that he had viewed this portrait in its unfinished state (Waingrow, 1994, p. 269). This viewing may have occurred on 16 April 1763, when he recorded in a memorandum his intention to visit Reynolds's studio (Lustig, 1987, pp. 173–74; Boswell, 2010, p. 201). Although his claim to have seen the portrait before meeting either Johnson or Reynolds has been challenged (Yung, 1984, p. 80; Folkenflik, 2014, p. 276), Boswell is unlikely to have erred on a matter of such importance.

Newspaper advertisements for the *Life* in the spring of 1791 would draw attention to the fact that this portrait was engraved "by Heath, from the large

Picture painted by Sir Joshua Reynolds in 1756, being the first, and never before engraved" (Figure 17). Boswell must have provided this information in response to a letter from Dilly of 22 March (Yale, C 1056), indicating that Heath, having "nearly finished his Portrait of Dr. Johnson," wanted to know the date of the painting and Johnson's age at that time. Dilly's letter then tells Boswell that "all this matter" should be explained "in the advertisement which you have entirely omitted" – from which we can infer that Boswell wrote much, if not all, the copy in the newspaper advertisements. Boswell added to the advertisements the date Reynolds painted (or at least started) the portrait but not Johnson's age at that time. What evidently mattered most to him was that the portrait was by Reynolds, that Reynolds had given it to him (as he also noted in the *Public Advertiser* on 18 June 1791 and in the text beneath the frontispiece itself), and that he could claim for it two firsts: the first-ever portrait of his subject and the first time it had ever been engraved.

After a fortuitous delay in transporting Reynolds's portrait saved it from being damaged or destroyed by a fire in Heath's home on Lisle Street (*Public Advertiser*, 24 March 1789; Heath, 1993), Heath secured the painting and made a stipple engraving from it – quite different from the line engraving he had done from Opie's portrait of Johnson (on stipple and line frontispiece engraving, see Sher, 2006, pp. 165–66). Four states or versions of Heath's engraving have survived (NPG 1597; Yung, 1984, pp. 79–83; Lustig, 1987). From the outset the engraving contained various accessories that were not present in the unfinished painting, including the first volume of Johnson's *Dictionary*, an inkwell, a second quill, and a wooden table. Since most of these accessories were eventually added to the painting itself with Reynolds's approval, it seems likely that they originated with Reynolds rather than Heath or Boswell. Reynolds unquestionably determined the next set of developments. According to remarks that Boswell placed beneath the second state of the engraving (which he thought was the first state), Heath, believing his work was finished, "went with me to Sir Joshua Reynolds's who suggested that the countenance was too young and not thoughtful enough. Mr. Heath therefore altered it so much to its advantage that Sir Joshua was quite satisfied, and Heath then saw such a difference that he said he would not for a hundred pounds have had it remain as it was" (Figure 15). Heath's engraving was transformed owing to Reynolds's instructions, and in the next (third) state, as in the almost identical frontispiece version (Figure 1a), Johnson's face does look older, more thoughtful, and more distinguished.

Boswell was delighted with the finished product. On the day after publication, he described it in a long newspaper puff that begins, "The engraved portrait of DR. JOHNSON, prefixed to MR. BOSWELL's life of that celebrated man, we must say,

Figure 15 The second state of Heath's frontispiece engraving, with Boswell's commentary. Houghton Library, Harvard University, MS Hyde 51 (25)

in justice to MR. HEATH, is one of the most capital performances that has appeared for some time" (Tankard, 2014, pp. 263–65). But we have seen that Reynolds, not Boswell, was chiefly responsible for the improvements Heath made. That Reynolds also approved of Heath's performance can be inferred from his subsequent patronage. On 10 November 1791 Heath would be appointed an associate engraver of the Royal Academy that Reynolds headed (Heath, ARA), paving the way for his appointment in 1794 as Historical Engraver to the King (Figure 13).

Heath was well rewarded for the effort he expended on his engraved portrait of Johnson: his fee of £47 5s. was more than any other single expense in the *Life* except paper and print. Dilly's impression account contains another item relating to the engraved portrait: "Hinton – Plate paper and working 1950 Heads – [£]19 10[s.] / Tissue paper for D[itt]o. –14[s.]" These were the charges for materials and labor for printing the frontispiece portrait, once Heath's engraving had been handed over to Dilly. That task was performed by the copperplate printer William Hinton, then situated in Horseshoe Alley, Ludgate Hill (Maxted, 1977,

p. 111). The term "working" refers to printing the portrait from the engraved plate, using a copperplate press and "Plate paper." Owing to the softness of copper and the large size of the print run, "working" may also have required retouching the plate during the printing process. Since 1,950 "Heads" were printed – 200 more than the book's print run – 200 prints of Johnson would have been available for distribution or sale (e.g., NPG D34873), but it is not known what Boswell did with them. Combining the fees paid to Heath and Hinton, the full cost to Boswell for the frontispiece portrait was £67 9s.

As Reynolds worked behind the scenes to bolster the frontispiece portrait, another of Boswell's close friends was the prime mover behind the second major engraving in the *Life of Johnson*. On 11 April 1776 Boswell invited Sir William Forbes to a supper at the Crown and Anchor Tavern with Johnson, Reynolds, and Langton. Forbes and his wife Elizabeth, Lady Forbes, already knew Langton well, and they became friendly with Reynolds and his niece and companion, Mary Palmer, when Reynolds painted their portraits that spring. Sometime after Boswell's departure for Edinburgh on 17 May, Forbes joined Langton, Burke, Barnard, and several others at a dinner party at Reynolds's home in Leicester Square. There they plotted to produce a group letter to Johnson requesting that he revise his epitaph for Oliver Goldsmith by improving his characterization as an author and by rendering it in English rather than Latin. Fearing Johnson's wrath, they playfully constructed their letter in the form of a round robin, like sailors engaged in a mutiny. Forbes was an outsider at this gathering, but having skill in lettering, he was chosen as the clerk or scribe, recording text written mainly by Burke. Reynolds subsequently presented the Round Robin to Johnson, who received it in good humor, though without practical effect. Barnard took the Round Robin home to Ireland, where it would have stayed if Forbes had not made a copy when he and his wife visited Barnard in Dublin in August 1785. Forbes told Boswell about it and sent him a copy on 18 October 1787. The next day he sent Boswell an account of the Round Robin's creation and informed him that the original document could be obtained from Barnard. At Boswell's request, following Forbes's suggestion, Barnard sent the original to Boswell for engraving in December 1790 (Sher, 2022, pp. 106 n. 51, 109–10).

Whereas the frontispiece required much time and effort by a skilled engraver, in consultation with the painter of the original portrait, the engraving of the Round Robin, like the engraving of Johnson's facsimile signatures, was relatively straightforward work, involving tracing and lettering rather than portrait artistry. For this reason, engraving both the Round Robin and Johnson's facsimile signatures brought the engraver, "H. Shepherd" – the "lettering engraver" Henry Shepherd (Alexander, 2021, p. 818) – just five guineas (£5 5s.). The only notable technical issue was a spacing problem that required Shepherd to abbreviate (or further abbreviate) the first names of Reynolds, Forbes, and Barnard at the bottom of the circle (Sher 2022, p. 108 n. 4). Both of Shepherd's engravings, like Heath's frontispiece portrait, bear the publication date 10 April 1791.

Unlike the frontispiece engraving, which needed no supporting text (other than the brief reference to it on the day Boswell met Johnson), the Round Robin required explanation. In the first edition of the *Life*, Boswell started the discussion with Johnson's twenty-line Latin epitaph for Goldsmith (Boswell, 1791b, 2:91–92). The way he secured the text of the epitaph shows his reliance on the competence and learning of Plymsell, whom he sent only the following curt instruction: "Take it in from Johnson's Poems & pray keep them unsullied" (Bonnell, 2012, p. 67 n. 4). Following the conclusion of the epitaph at the top of page 92, instead of telling the story of the Round Robin in his own words, Boswell inserted most of Forbes's letter of 19 October 1787 (though without the date of the letter or the season of the event), set off by the words "Sir William Forbes writes to me thus:" After the last line of the long excerpt from Forbes's letter – "I consider this *Round Robin* as a species of literary curiosity worth preserving, as it marks, in a certain degree, Dr. Johnson's character" – Boswell introduced what he called "a faithful transcript" of the Round Robin itself, placed on the next page. Readers of the first edition would therefore encounter the story of the Round Robin and a reproduction of it in the same visual field (Figure 16a; Sher, 2022, pp. 101–7 & notes).

The Round Robin segment concludes on the next page, with one paragraph expounding on the final quotation from Forbes's letter, beginning "Sir William Forbes's observation is very just" (Sher, forthcoming), and another paragraph contending that the text of the Round Robin demonstrates Burke's versatility as a writer (Boswell, 1791b, 2:93). The segment serves as one example among many of how the *Life of Johnson* expanded beyond its original one-volume length because of Boswell's tireless search for additional material and the assistance he received from his support network. Like the frontispiece, the engravings of the Round Robin and Johnson's facsimile signatures had to be "worked" on plate paper and a copperplate press and, as always, the costs were passed on to Boswell in Dilly's impression account: "Smith [i.e., John Smith, copperplate printer in King's Head Court, Shoe Lane (Maxted 1977, p. 208)] – Working the round Robin and the Fac Simile 1750 each – @ 2/6 [i.e. 2s. 6d.] – [£]4 7[s.] 6[d.] / 1¾ R[ea]m Super Royal paper for D[itt]o – [£]3 10[s.]" With these additional expenses, the cost of engraving and printing the Round Robin and signature facsimiles was £13 2s. 6d., and the total charge for all three engravings was £80 11s. 6d.

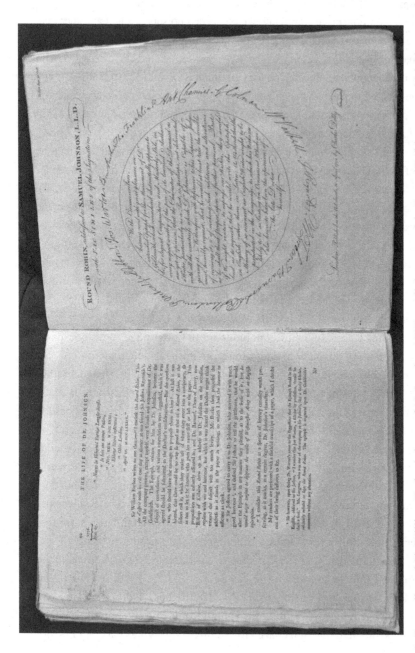

Figure 16a Boswell used Sir William Forbes's letter of 19 October 1787 to tell the story of the Round Robin on page 92 in the second volume of the first edition, opposite an engraving of the Round Robin itself. Beinecke Rare Book and Manuscript Library, Yale University

> 92
> 1776.
> Ætat. 67.
>
> THE LIFE OF DR. JOHNSON.
>
> " *Natus in Hibernia Forniæ Longfordienfis.*
> " *In loco cui nomen Pallas,*
> " *Nov.* XXIX. M DCC XXXI ;
> " *Eblanæ literis inftitutus ;*
> " *Obiit Londini,*
> " *April* IV. M DCC LXXXIV."
>
> Sir William Forbes writes to me thus :—" I enclofe the *Round Robin*. This *jeu d'efprit* took its rife one day at dinner at our friend Sir Jofhua Reynolds's. All the company prefent, except myfelf, were friends and acquaintance of Dr. Goldfmith. The Epitaph, written for him by Dr. Johnfon, became the fubject of converfation, and various emendations were fuggefted, which it was agreed fhould be fubmitted to the Doctor's confideration.—But the queftion was, who fhould have the courage to propofe them to him ? At laft it was hinted, that there could be no way fo good as that of a *Round Robin*, as the failors call it, which they make ufe of when they enter into a confpiracy, fo as not to let it be known who puts his name firft or laft to the paper. This propofition was inftantly affented to ; and Dr. Barnard, Dean of Derry, now Bifhop of Killaloe, drew up an addrefs to Dr. Johnfon on the occafion, replete with wit and humour, but which it was feared the Doctor might think treated the fubject with too much levity. Mr. Burke then propofed the addrefs as it ftands in the paper in writing, to which I had the honour to officiate as clerk.
>
> " Sir Jofhua agreed to carry it to Dr. Johnfon, who received it with much good humour [7], and defired Sir Jofhua to tell the gentlemen, that he would alter the Epitaph in any manner they pleafed, as to the fenfe of it ; but *he would never confent to difgrace the walls of Weftminfter Abbey with an Englifh infcription.*
>
> " I confider this *Round Robin* as a fpecies of literary curiofity worth pre-ferving, as it marks, in a certain degree, Dr. Johnfon's character."
>
> My readers are prefented with a faithful tranfcript of a paper, which I doubt not of their being defirous to fee.
>
> ---
>
> [7] He however, upon feeing Dr. Warton's name to the fuggeftion that the Epitaph fhould be in Englifh, obferved to Sir Jofhua, " I wonder that Joe Warton, a fcholar by profeffion, fhould be fuch a fool." Mr. Langton, who was one of the company at Sir Jofhua's, like a fturdy fcholar, refolutely refufed to fign the *Round Robin*. The epitaph is engraved upon Dr. Goldfmith's monument without any alteration.
>
> Sir

Figure 16b Detail of page 92 from Figure 16a. Beinecke Rare Book and Manuscript Library, Yale University. For other images of the Round Robin and a transcription of the encircled text, see Sher, 2022, pp. 107–11.

3.2.3 Stationers' Hall

We have seen that nine copies of the *Life* in sheets were sent to Stationers' Hall to register the book, and the same was done with the *Letter to Chesterfield* and the *Conversation* (each printed on a single sheet of paper). As the fee for registering a publication at Stationers' Hall was sixpence regardless of its format, size, or number of volumes, Dilly's impression account records "Entering the Work at Stationer's Hall and also the two single sheets. – 1[s.] 6 [d.]" (i.e., eighteen pence).

3.2.4 Advertising, Boarding, Transporting, Warehousing

Dilly's impression account charges Boswell £11 9s. for "Advertising in the London papers." The first known advertisement appeared in the *London Chronicle* on 19 March 1791, with the correct price but erroneous information about the timing (*"Next month will be published"*) (Tankard, 2014, pp. 258–59). When this advertisement was repeated on 31 March, the publication date was changed to "in a few days" and new text was added about the three engravings. These March advertisements contained a paragraph attributing the unavoidable delay of the work to its "enlargement" owing to the "extraordinary zeal" shown "by distinguished persons in all parts of the kingdom, in supplying additional information, authentic manuscripts, and singular Anecdotes of Dr. Johnson." It is possible to pinpoint the day when publication was set for 16 May (the thirty-eighth anniversary of Boswell's first meeting with Johnson), because a blurb in the *Morning Chronicle* on 28 April anticipates publication "in six or eight days," but two days later the correct publication date appears in an advertisement in the *London Chronicle*. That advertisement also contains a pitch for the third edition of the *Tour*, embellished with a new map dated 10 April 1791, "describing the route of the Travellers," which could be purchased separately for sixpence (Pottle, 1929, pp. 122, 167). Although Pottle believed that London newspaper advertising for the *Life of Johnson* "disappears" after an advertisement in the *London Chronicle* (and other newspapers) on 7 May, another prepublication advertisement appeared on 14 May in the *Public Advertiser*, *Times*, and *St. James's Chronicle* (Figure 17), and advertisements headed "This Day is Published," or similar, continued to appear in the London newspapers (e.g., *World*, 3 June; *Morning Post*, 7 June).

These advertisements make it possible to chart changes in the publicity for the *Life*, and perhaps also the book's full title, as Boswell wrestled with these issues around the time of publication. Some of the changes were slight. In the March advertisements, the word "Also" was used to introduce the phrase "various Pieces of his Composition," but in response to Malone's plea in a letter to Boswell of 14 April that the title page should "not admit ... that heavy word *also*" (Baker, 1986, pp. 417–18), the word "And" was substituted. The change of the word "*Containing*" to "*Comprehending*" in the title (suggested by John Taylor, as previously noted) predated all the

> On *Monday the* 16th *of May will be publiſhed,*.
> In Two Volumes, Quarto, Price Two Guineas, in Boards,
>   (Dedicated to Sir JOSHUA REYNOLDS,)
>   And illuſtrated with the following Plates:
> Dr. JOHNSON, by HEATH, from the large Picture painted
>   by Sir JOSHUA REYNOLDS in 1756, being the firſt,
>   and never before engraved; Fac Similes of his H·nd-
>   writing at different Periods; and a Round Rob'n addreſſed
>   to him concerning his Epitaph on Dr. Goldſmith.
> **THE LIFE of SAMUEL JOHNSON, LL.D.**
>   Comprehend'ng an Account of his Studies and nume-
> rous Works in Chronological Order; a Series of his Epiſto-
> lary Correſpondence and Converſations with many eminent
> Perſons; including his Converſation with THE KING;
> and his celebrated Letter to the Earl of CHESTERFIELD,;
> and various Pieces of his Compoſition, never before publiſhed.
> The Whole exhibiting a VIEW of LITERATURE and
> LITERARY MEN in Great-Britain, for near half a Cen-
> tury, during which he flouriſhed.
>   By JAMES BOSWELL, Eſq.
>   London: Printed for Charles Dilly, in the Poultry.
> *⁎⁎* The extraordinary Zeal which has been ſhown by
> diſtinguiſhed Perſons in all Quarters, in ſupplying additional
> Information, authentick Manuſcripts, and ſingu'ar Anec-
> dotes of Dr. Johnſon, has occaſioned ſuch an Enlargement
> of this Work, that it has been unavoidably delayed much
> longer than was intended.
>   At the ſame time will be publiſhed, by Charles Dilly,
>   The JOURNAL of a TOUR to the HEBRIDES with
> SAMUEL JOHNSON, LL.D. The 3d Edi·. co rected.
> To which is now add·d, a MAP deſcribing the Route of the
> Travellers.
>   N. B. The Map, Price 6d. may be had ſeparately, to
> accommodate the Purchaſers of the former Editions.

Figure 17 Advertisement for the first edition in the *St. James's Chronicle*, 14 May 1791. Burney Newspapers Collection

advertisements. A more substantive alteration involved Johnson's letter to Chesterfield and conversation with the king. The advertisement on 19 March touts Johnson's "celebrated Letter to the Earl of CHESTERFIELD" but does not mention the royal interview (Tankard, 2014, pp. 258–59; Baker, 1986, p. 415). The 7 May advertisement omits both the Chesterfield letter and the royal interview and gives the full title of the book in its final form, as in Figure 1b. Yet the last prepublication advertisement on 14 May contains the phrase "including his Conversation with THE KING; and his celebrated Letter to the Earl of CHESTERFIELD" as if it were part of the title, and this phrase would remain in the advertisements that followed publication.

The next charge for London advertising is unexpected: "D[itt]o as forwarding for the press in 1787 – [£]2 5[s.]." This item refers to the bulky paragraph that appeared in the *Public Advertiser* (21 May 1787), *London Chronicle* (22 May), *The World* (31 May), the front page of the

June issue of the *Gentleman's Magazine*, and possibly elsewhere. It begins, "The Public are respectfully informed, that Mr. BOSWELL'S LIFE OF DR. JOHNSON is in great forwardness" (Pottle, 1929, p. 163; Tankard, 2014, p. 241). The gist of it is that Boswell supposedly expected "to obtain much information" from "some other publications" (meaning the books on Johnson by Hawkins and Piozzi) but has been "disappointed," and will "correct these erroneous accounts" in his forthcoming work. The impression account reveals that Dilly had paid for this early advertisement and had not forgotten to pass the cost along to Boswell four years later. But Dilly did not charge Boswell for the two-page teaser for his forthcoming "literary monument" to Johnson (said to be "in the Press") at the back of *A Catalogue of Books Printed for, and Sold by Charles Dilly, in London* (1787).

The impression account records "Paid for Advertising 7 Times in the Edinburgh papers – [£]2 18[s.]" The first notice I have found in the Edinburgh press is a small advertisement by William Gordon and N. R. Cheyne in both the *Edinburgh Evening Courant* and *Caledonian Mercury* on 26 May 1791, headed "*Just published, and lately arrived.*" Books published in London usually appeared a little later in Scotland, and the gap of about ten days in this instance was not unusual. Other advertisements in the *Caledonian Mercury* by William Creech (28 May) and Peter Hill (6 June) list *The Life of Samuel Johnston* among their other titles – Scottifying Johnson's surname in a manner that Boswell said Johnson "could not bear" (Boswelliana, Yale, M 38). The large, authorized advertisements that Dilly charged to Boswell began appearing in late May (e.g., *Edinburgh Advertiser*, 27 May; *Edinburgh Evening Courant*, 28 May; *Caledonian Mercury*, 9 June). The text was similar to the advertisement in the *London Chronicle* on 31 March 1791, including information about the volumes, format, price, dedication, engravings, and imprint ("London, printed for Charles Dilly"), with the paragraph about the delayed publication as a result of the book's "enlargement" and an approximation of the full title as it may have stood at that time – including the word "Also" and the reference to Johnson's "celebrated Letters [*sic*] to the Earl of Chesterfield" but not to the interview with the king (Figure 18). The differences occur at the top, where the statement about publication occurring "in a few days" is replaced by "THIS DAY IS PUBLISHED," followed by a list of local sales agents: John Bell and John Bradfute (trading as Bell & Bradfute), William Creech, Elphinston Balfour, Peter Hill, Thomas Duncan, John and James Fairbairn (trading as J. & J. Fairbairn), and Alexander Guthrie. The copies for sale were apparently sent by Dilly to Guthrie's shop at 25 South Bridge, for distribution to the other participating Scottish booksellers. Although it is not

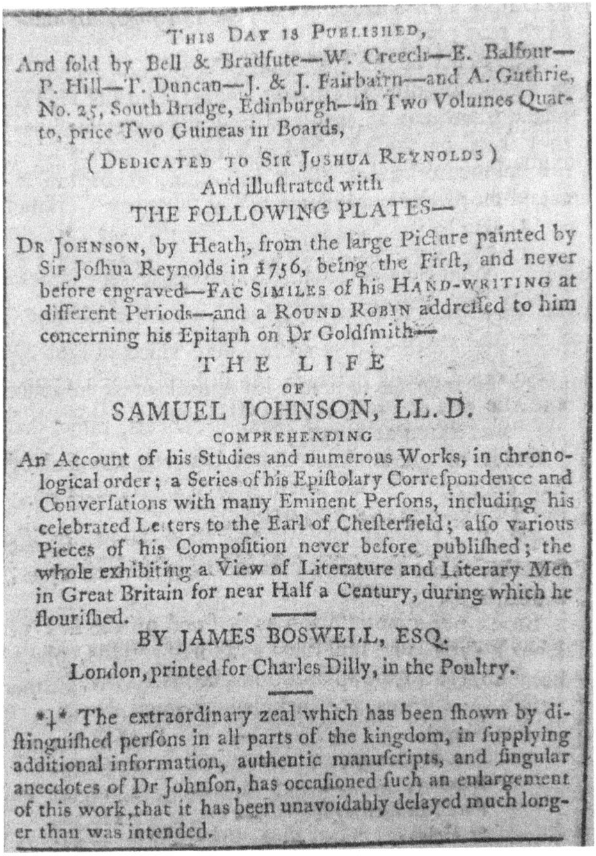

THIS DAY IS PUBLISHED,

And ſold by Bell & Bradſute—W. Creech—E. Balfour—P. Hill—T. Duncan—J. & J. Fairbairn—and A. Guthrie, No. 25, South Bridge, Edinburgh—In Two Volumes Quarto, price Two Guineas in Boards,

(DEDICATED TO SIR JOSHUA REYNOLDS)

And illuſtrated with

THE FOLLOWING PLATES—

DR JOHNSON, by Heath, from the large Picture painted by Sir Joſhua Reynolds in 1756, being the Firſt, and never before engraved—FAC SIMILES of his HAND-WRITING at different Periods—and a ROUND ROBIN addreſſed to him concerning his Epitaph on Dr Goldſmith—

THE LIFE

OF

SAMUEL JOHNSON, LL.D.

COMPREHENDING

An Account of his Studies and numerous Works, in chronological order; a Series of his Epiſtolary Correſpondence and Converſations with many Eminent Perſons, including his celebrated Letters to the Earl of Cheſterfield; alſo various Pieces of his Compoſition never before publiſhed; the whole exhibiting a View of Literature and Literary Men in Great Britain for near Half a Century, during which he flouriſhed.

BY JAMES BOSWELL, ESQ.

London, printed for Charles Dilly, in the Poultry.

‡ The extraordinary zeal which has been ſhown by diſtinguiſhed perſons in all parts of the kingdom, in ſupplying additional information, authentic manuſcripts, and ſingular anecdotes of Dr Johnſon, has occaſioned ſuch an enlargement of this work, that it has been unavoidably delayed much longer than was intended.

Figure 18 Dilly charged Boswell for seven advertisements in the Edinburgh newspapers, including this one in the *Edinburgh Evening Courant*, 28 May 1791. National Library of Scotland

known how Gordon and Cheyne got a jump on the authorized Edinburgh sellers, a likely explanation is that they were supplied surreptitiously by one of the London booksellers who had purchased many copies at Dilly's trade sale. We shall see that the advertisements that Boswell purchased in the Edinburgh newspapers would do little to increase authorized sales of the first edition of the *Life* in Scotland.

All told, Boswell was charged £16 12s. for advertising the first edition of the *Life* in London and Edinburgh. These charges do not include the numerous "news" items and puffs in the newspapers, which often provided free publicity for him and his book. Although it has been claimed that the London newspapers "classified puffs as advertisements and charged for them accordingly" (Werkmeister, 1963, p. 7), Boswell could rely on friendly organs such as the

Public Advertiser, St. James's Chronicle, and *Gentleman's Magazine* to print the items he gave them at no charge (Baker, 1986, pp. 302, 318; Tankard, 2021, p. 34). It should not be forgotten, however, that several other newspapers were filled with criticism and mockery of Boswell and his book, and "the Gang" was constantly on guard. "No man is honoured with more abuse than Jemmy Boswell," cracked the *World* on 26 July 1792 (quoted in Werkmeister, 1963, p. 48).

The impression account concludes with a variety of lesser charges. First, Dilly charged Boswell two shillings per set for "Boarding 49 Presentation Copies," for a total of £4 18s. There is a slight discrepancy here, since 4 of the 52 copies that Boswell claimed for his own use (whether for himself or as presentation copies) were listed in the impression account as being in "sheets" rather than "boards," leaving 48 copies to be boarded, rather than 49. The remaining charges relate to transportation and storage, a category of expenses that is sometimes neglected by book historians. It cost 1s. 10d. to transport presentation copies to Capel Lofft and Bishop Douglas, who lived a distance from London. A charge of fourteen shillings for "Freight to and from Edinburgh," though placed in the advertising section of Dilly's impression account, apparently refers to the cost of sending 40 copies to Edinburgh – 2 presentation copies and 38 copies for sale there – as well as the cost of returning 18 of those copies to London booksellers, as recorded on 17 May 1791 (Yale, A 60, f. 180). Dilly charged one pound for "Cartage and Helper to Deliver the subscription Copies," meaning the copies purchased by booksellers at the trade sale in the spring and summer of 1791, as discussed in the next section. He charged another pound for "Cartage of the Remainder of the Impression [i.e., the unsold copies] to my warehouse & helper." The five charges I have grouped together under the heading transportation and storage came to a total of £7 13s. 10d.

And there it was: £943 16s. 4d. in charges that Boswell owed Dilly for the cost of printing, publishing, advertising, selling, delivering, and warehousing the first edition. It was certainly a "monstrous" list of expenses and deductions, but the costs resulted from Boswell's own decisions about the book's format and number of volumes, print run, paper and type, corrections and cancels, overrun pamphlets, engravings, advertisements, and presentation copies.

4 Selling the First Edition

On Friday 13 May 1791 Boswell sent Sir William Forbes a letter containing this celebratory paragraph:

> My Life of Dr. Johnson is at length fairly launched; though the formal day of publication is not till monday. Considering that *two volumes Quarto price two*

guineas must give pause, I have no reason to be discouraged. *This day* my volumes are purchased by *forty one booksellers of London*, to the amount of *upwards of four hundred*; and one of them who received twenty sets in the morning has sent word that they are all sold and has got ten more. This opening besides Scotland Ireland and various Country towns promises well. Scotland I do not expect to do much; and Ireland still less. But the general curiosity of this extensive and opulent country is wonderful. (Sher, 2022, p. 219)

Later in the letter he adds: "I am as you may suppose, very busy at my Bookseller's." The *Life of Johnson* would not be published until Monday 16 May, and yet Boswell states that more than 400 copies had already been sold by the preceding Friday. How? To whom? And why was Boswell "very busy" at Dilly's bookshop?

4.1 The London Trade Sale

The year and a half between Boswell's letter to Forbes on 13 May 1791 and the final settlement with Dilly and Baldwin in mid-November 1792 is in most respects disappointing for information about Boswell's life and work. Until 29 October 1792 Boswell kept no journal during this period except while traveling away from London. His surviving letters are not plentiful (e.g., Waingrow, 2001, pp. 313–88), and he no longer maintained a register of his correspondence. Most of what we know paints a grim picture of his personal circumstances. Several "matrimonial schemes" had gone awry, he informed Temple on 22 August 1791. Three months later he told Temple that a visit to Auchinleck from late August to mid-October, the first since the death of his wife in 1789, brought back sad memories and sunk him into "languor and gloom," and his "depression of spirits … continued" after his return to London (Tinker, 1924, 2:439–41). He was now well aware that his career as an English barrister was a failure, as were his efforts to obtain preferment through political channels. The death of Sir Joshua Reynolds on 23 February 1792 was devastating and broke up "the Gang." His drinking problem worsened. His work on the second edition of the *Life* has been characterized as "desultory" (Danziger & Brady, 1989, p. 155).

There was, however, one uplifting activity during this period. On 12–13 May 1791 Dilly began wholesaling the printed sheets of the first edition of the *Life of Johnson* to the London book trade, and Boswell, as the book's publisher, was heavily involved. Indeed, the only surviving sales record comes from lists that are almost entirely in his handwriting, as well as summaries drawn from those lists in his personal correspondence.

Figure 19 reproduces Boswell's record of the opening days of the trade sale. The document is titled "Subscription Boswell's Life of Johnson 2 Vols Q[uar]to sub[scribe]d. at £1.12.0 Kept at £1.14.0. Sells a[t] £2 2 0 in boards." This means that the wholesale price was £1 12s. in sheets (or two shillings more if a purchaser wished to store copies in Dilly's warehouse), and the retail price was two guineas in boards. As discussed earlier, the wholesale income belonged entirely to Boswell in his capacity as publisher; retail booksellers took their profit from the difference between the wholesale price in sheets and the retail price in boards (i.e., ten shillings, minus their cost for boarding each set). Next come the terms: "40 sets & upwards to be paid by notes at 6 & 9 months – under that number by one note at six months." Thus, volume sales gave purchasers better payment terms but no discount in the price. After the date, "12 & 13 May" (considered as one "day"), Boswell lists the booksellers along with the number of sets they purchased. The information in this list corroborates his hurried letter to Forbes on the 13th. Boswell told Forbes that forty-one booksellers had made purchases "*This day*"; his list contains forty-three names, suggesting that the last two placed their orders after he wrote the letter. He told Forbes that upward of 400 copies had been sold; the actual number he recorded was 431. He told Forbes that one bookseller who purchased 20 copies in the morning ordered 10 more that afternoon because the first batch "are all sold." He was evidently referring to Robert Faulder at 42 New Bond Street, who purchased a total of 30 sets on the first day. This anecdote establishes that sales to retail purchasers began well before the "official" publication date on the 16th. The scene at Dilly's bookshop must have been noisy and exciting, as the booksellers or their clerks registered their orders, knowing that they needed to move quickly to install boards so that copies would be ready for their customers the following week. Boswell was in the thick of it.

Forty-nine more copies were sold on the second day, Saturday 14 May, including an additional ten to Faulder. Nearly all those forty-nine copies went to booksellers who can be presumed to have sold their initial purchases from the 13th (Boswell marked the times they returned with a circled number at this stage of his reporting, though he later dropped this practice). The 14th was also the day on which the final prepublication advertisement for the *Life* appeared in the London newspapers, headed "*On Monday the 16th of May will be published*" (Figure 17). Although the prepublication surge of sales to the trade subsided after the book officially went on sale on the 16th, over the next several months the leading booksellers sold their copies and came back for more, while others made their first (and sometimes only) purchases. We cannot be sure how often Boswell was actually in Dilly's bookshop recording daily sales, but his continued involvement is demonstrated by the existence of the daily sales

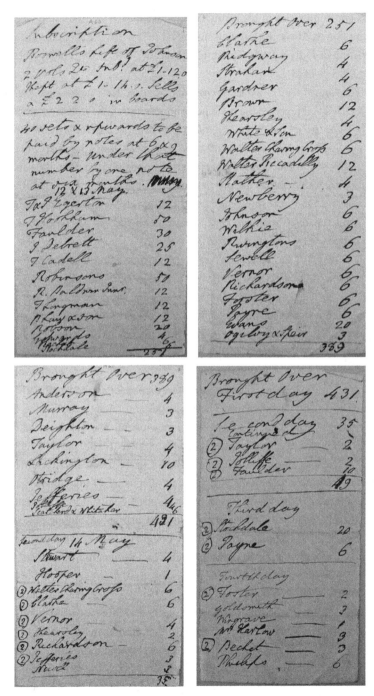

Figure 19 The first four pages of Boswell's record of sales of the first edition at Dilly's London trade sale, which began on 12–13 May 1791. Beinecke Rare Book and Manuscript Library, Yale University, A 60

records and summaries in his handwriting – except for the first three weeks of his excursion to Auchinleck in late summer 1791, when the accounts are in the handwriting of Dilly's clerk, Christopher Ingram (Yale, A 60; Pottle, Abbott & Pottle, 1993, 3:1113–14).

On 22 August 1791, as he prepared to depart for Auchinleck the next morning, Boswell reported the good news about sales of the *Life* in an otherwise gloomy letter to Temple: "My *Magnum Opus* sells wonderfully. 1200 are now gone, and we hope the whole 1700 may be gone before Christmas" (Tinker, 1924, 2:439–40). It had certainly been a strong opening run, with 506 sets sold to the London trade before the official date of publication and about 700 more total sales over the next three months. But Boswell's hopes of unloading the entire print run by Christmas 1791 were unrealistic. As we have seen, that barely happened by Christmas 1792.

Table 1 displays the cumulative sales of the first edition of the *Life* to the London book trade up to the time Boswell stopped keeping daily records on 13 June 1792. By then, sixty-three London booksellers had purchased more than 1,400 sets. The table shows the names and locations of the top twenty-five purchasers. Not surprisingly, the family firm of George Robinson, who had offered to buy the copyright before publication, took by far the most copies. Robinson's firm, like Thomas Hookham, subscribed for 50 copies on the first day of the sale, demonstrating that these booksellers had both sufficient capital (£80 for 50 sets at the wholesale price) and enough confidence in the book's marketability to make a large initial investment. The Robinsons returned twenty-eight more times over the next eleven months, usually purchasing 6 sets on each occasion. Hookham returned only six more times after the first day, suggesting that he had a more difficult time disposing of his copies. Faulder started somewhat slower with 30 sets but was subsequently more persistent than Hookham and eventually passed him. A more conservative buying policy was followed by the "Rivingtons," who initially bought just 6 copies but returned ten more times, usually taking 6 copies on each trip, to finish fourth with a total of 57 sets by 13 June 1792.

By that date, the Robinsons, Hookham, and Faulder together had purchased 394 copies – almost a quarter of the 1,689 sets put up for sale. The twenty-five firms identified in Table 1 accounted for 1,158, or more than 68 percent, of those 1,689 copies by then, and the London trade as a whole took 1,401 copies, or 83 percent of the total. As discussed in what follows, by the time all 1,689 sets were sold in November 1792, the proportion of sales to the London booksellers was probably around 87 percent, or more than 90 percent, if Dilly's own purchases (in his capacity as a retail bookseller) are included. The London book trade reigned supreme.

Table 1 The Top Twenty-Five Purchasers of the First Edition
(through 13 June 1792)

Bookseller or Firm	Location	Sets Purchased
"Robinsons" (George Robinson I and family)	Paternoster Row	212
Robert Faulder	New Bond Street	100
Thomas Hookham	New Bond Street	82
"Rivingtons" (John Rivington I and family)	St. Paul's Churchyard	57
John Debrett	Piccadilly	53
James Lackington	Chiswell Street	52
John Stockdale (including 25 copies noted in Table 2)	Piccadilly	51
Bedwell Law & Son (Charles Law)	Ave Maria Lane	50
Thomas Longman	Paternoster Row	48
John Sewell	Cornhill	47
William Richardson	Cornhill	40
John Walter	Charing Cross	39
Thomas Evans	Paternoster Row	34
Thomas Cadell Sr.	Strand	33
Robert Baldwin (and Robert Baldwin Jr.)	Paternoster Row	32
John Payne	Paternoster Row	31
James Robson	New Bond Street	29
Henry Lasher Gardner	Strand	24
Thomas Vernor	Birchin Lane (Cornhill)	24
James Edwards	Pall Mall	23
William Brown	Strand	21
John Murray I	Fleet Street	21
Thomas and John Egerton	Charing Cross	20
Edward Jeffery	Pall Mall	19
Joseph Johnson	St. Paul's Churchyard	16
SUBTOTAL		1,158
38 others with 15 or fewer purchases		243
TOTAL		**1,401**

Source: Beinecke Rare Book and Manuscript Library, Yale University, A 60

Among the leading purchasers of the first edition were several individuals with whom Boswell was connected. Faulder, the second largest purchaser, had published Boswell's bizarre anonymous pamphlet, *No Abolition of Slavery; or the Universal Empire of Love: A Poem*, just one month before the *Life* appeared. John Sewell was, like Isaac Reed, one of the three proprietors of the *European Magazine*, which promoted the *Life* and its author. Thomas Cadell Sr. – who would soon give way to his son Thomas Jr. and his foreman William Davies, trading as Cadell & Davies – was the successor of Andrew Millar and the publishing partner of the late William Strahan, both of whom played roles in Johnson's life and Boswell's biography. Strahan's son and successor Andrew, who had inherited his father's unusual status as a printer entitled to attend the London trade sales, purchased 10 copies of the first edition (including 4 shown in Figure 19). Boswell recorded that 12 copies were sold on the first day of the sale to "R. Baldwin Junr."; this was Henry's eldest son, Robert, who was employed by Henry's brother, the bookseller Robert Baldwin Sr. (who took 32 copies in all), until his premature death in September 1791 at the age of twenty-four. Many of the other purchasers of the first edition also had ties to Dilly, with whom Boswell was so closely associated. It was a tight-knit fraternity of bookmen. "Mrs. Harlow" – Elizabeth Harlow, a bookseller's widow (Maxted, 1977, p. 102) – who ordered 9 sets in the spring of 1791 (the first 3 on 16 May, as shown in Figure 19), was the only female bookseller to purchase copies at Dilly's trade sale, bearing out one scholar's assertion that "To be a woman in [the book] business in this period, even as a widow, was to be an anomaly" (Grundy, 2009, p. 151).

Many of the booksellers whose names appear in Table 1 were based in the traditional heart of the London "bookscape" in the old City of London, centered in Paternoster Row and St. Paul's Churchyard, and extending from the Fleet Street area in the west to the Cornhill area in the east (Raven, 2014). Table 1 also shows the westward expansion of the London book trade during the late eighteenth and early nineteenth centuries (Raven, 2007, pp. 185–90). The shops of eleven of the twenty-five leading purchasers of the first edition were located west of Fleet Street: in The Strand, Charing Cross, Pall Mall, Piccadilly, and New Bond Street. In fact, the booksellers with premises in those streets subscribed for more copies of the first edition than the booksellers in Paternoster Row and St. Paul's Churchyard, and the combined sales to the three booksellers located in New Bond Street – Hookham, Faulder, and Faulder's former master James Robson – were equal to the purchases made by the Robinsons. For an expensive literary quarto, increasingly large numbers of buyers were to be found in the fashionable residential neighborhoods where lawyers and other professionals lived. The London booksellers were following the money.

4.2 Other Sales

Although London booksellers dominated Dilly's sales of the first edition, they were not the only purchasers. Boswell also reported Dilly's sales to booksellers in other locations and to retail customers. On 17 May 1791 he recorded that 44 copies had been sold to "Oxford & other Towns," as well as 6 sets to "Quakers" – a category that does not reappear in his records. On 7 July 1791 he registered another summary of sales mainly outside London: 76 "Country & Irish Sale," 29 "Single," 60 "Edinburgh say," and 4 sets to "Nunn & Coghlan," two London booksellers (James Nunn and James Peter Coghlan, the premier Roman Catholic printer and bookseller in London) who were, without explanation, kept separate from the rest of the London trade.

Table 2 reproduces a more comprehensive sales summary that Boswell recorded nine months later. It shows that 1,365 copies had been wholesaled to London booksellers by 4 April 1792 (including 31 copies that were logged separately: 25 "not marked" to John Stockdale in Piccadilly and 6 to Nunn and Coghlan). Since London booksellers would buy 1,401 sets by 13 June, as shown in Table 1, it seems that sales to the London trade had slowed to an average of a set every other day, or 15 per month, during the spring of 1792. Table 2 also demonstrates that the London booksellers (excluding the "Single" copies sold by Dilly himself) made more than 87 percent of the wholesale purchases as of early April 1792.

What of the other purchasers of the first edition? Under the category "Single," Boswell kept a record of daily sales to individual customers who bought copies in Dilly's shop, reaching a total of 50 by 4 April 1792, and 51 by the time he stopped

Table 2 "On 4 April [1792] Total Sale"

Purchasers	Sets Purchased
London Trade	1,334
Single	50
Dublin & Country	96
Edinburgh	52
Stockdale not marked	25
Nunn & Coghlan	6
Total as of 4 April 1792	**1,563**

Source: Beinecke Rare Book and Manuscript Library, Yale University, A 60

tabulating these kinds of sales on 10 May (Yale, A 61). As noted previously, the retail profit on these "Single" copies belonged to Dilly. If it cost him two shillings to put each of these sets in boards (the fee he charged Boswell for boarding), he would have earned a retail profit of eight shillings per set, or twenty pounds on the sale of 50 retail copies. A few more single sales must have occurred in the final six months of Dilly's sale, from May to November 1792. There are also oddities in Boswell's recording system, such as one occasion in which a "single" purchaser is identified by name (Boswell's friend "Ald[erman William] Curtis" on 12 July 1791). On another occasion, 17 December 1791, Boswell ambiguously reports 3 copies sold to "Stationers ready money."

In the letter to Forbes quoted at the beginning of Section 4, Boswell mentions "Scotland Ireland and various Country towns" as supplementary to the sales to the London trade, adding, "Scotland I do not expect to do much; and Ireland still less." We have seen that on 7 July 1791 Boswell estimated that 60 copies would be sold to the Edinburgh trade, but the reality – 52 copies as of 4 April 1792 – seems to have fallen short of even that modest goal. In a letter to Hugh Blair in Edinburgh on 3 November 1792, Boswell wrote: "I am sorry to say Scotland took only about 50; so virulent is Caledonian prejudice against Johnson" (Yale, L 62.2, draft). As a self-conscious Scot striving for assimilation in London, Boswell never fully comprehended why so few of his countrymen shared his enthusiasm for an Englishman who had repeatedly insulted them as a nation.

Boswell's prediction of "still less" from sales to Dublin proved accurate. Only 14 copies of the first edition went to Dublin on the first day of the trade sale in May 1791 and 4 more over the course of the next year (all on 7 July 1791), for a total of just 18 copies by 10 May 1792. Boswell's low expectations were rooted in awareness that the Dublin booksellers could be expected to issue their own, less expensive edition of any London literary work with strong commercial potential. When the *Tour* was being published in 1785, Boswell appeared to welcome this practice: he sent the printed sheets of the London first edition to Thomas Barnard in Dublin in order to facilitate an edition there, though he would receive no income from it, and he even took the extraordinary step of ensuring that revisions he made in the second edition to placate one disgruntled individual would be inserted into the unsold copies of the Dublin reprint as a cancel leaf (Sher, 2022, pp. 57 n. 11, 348–49). The quarto format and high price of the *Life* made it fairer game for a cheaper Dublin reprint than the *Tour*. Yet the Dublin edition of the *Life* appeared fifteen months after publication of the London quarto, as opposed to the mere six weeks it took for a reprint of the *Tour* to appear in Dublin after its publication in London. How can this difference be explained?

In February 1792 Patrick Byrne, a prominent Dublin bookseller who had co-published the Dublin edition of the *Tour* in November 1785, praised the *Life of Johnson* effusively in his *Universal Magazine and Review* and reported that it was "now printing in Dublin" (quoted in Cole, 1986, pp. 106, 108). What appeared in Dublin that month, however, was a reprint not of Boswell's complete *Life* but of an obscure two-volume 1791 London work by "Sir Andrew Anecdote" called *A Collection of Interesting Biography*. It featured a "revised and abridged" version of the *Life* in its first 183 pages, followed by shorter abridged biographies of John Elwes and Captain James Cook. The last page of the Boswell abridgment is a lengthy panegyric on "the very ingenious, accurate, minute, and learned Biographer," which concludes with this sentence: "On the whole, we have nothing to regret, but that the preceding Abridgment gives too faint an idea of the astonishing merit of the original" (p. 183). Boswell was probably not very concerned about an unauthorized abridgment that was this complimentary, and he therefore may not have minded when it was reissued separately in London under the pseudonym F. Thomas (Thomas, 1792; Pottle, 1929, pp. 196–99).

When Byrne, Richard Cross, and ten other Dublin booksellers, including most of those who had reprinted *A Collection of Interesting Biography*, finally produced their edition of the complete *Life of Johnson* in three octavo volumes on 21 August 1792 (Figure 3) – at about half the price of the London quarto first edition (£1 2s. 9d. bound, as advertised in the *Dublin Chronicle* on 23 August 1792) – the Irish public had been well primed to receive it. Despite being "not very accurately printed," the Dublin edition was "very generally demanded, and Universally Esteemed," according to one Irish correspondent (Waingrow, 2001, p. 382; see also p. 449), and would be among the works of eighteenth-century English literature most frequently found in Irish libraries and exported to America (Cole, 1986, pp. 29, 107). The images of the Round Robin and the facsimiles of Johnson's signatures were apparently reproduced by tracing the originals from the London first edition, with some alterations. They had to be folded because they originally had been made for a quarto rather than an octavo size. But the frontispiece engraving of Johnson could not be reproduced so easily or so cheaply. Its absence from the Dublin edition gave rise to a ludicrous error: the text of the Dublin edition retained Boswell's discussion of Reynolds's portrait, "from which an engraving has been made for this work" (Boswell, 1792, 1:323).

Despite the expectation of a cheaper Irish reprint, Boswell made at least one attempt to stimulate the Irish sale of the London first edition in advance of its publication. On 12 March 1791 he wrote to Malone, then in Dublin, "Pray could not you be of some service to my Work, by inquiring whether some of the Irish Booksellers would not take some" (Baker, 1986, p. 416). Malone's reply on 14 April explained that the Dublin booksellers "make it a rule never to advertise an English Work when they mean to reprint, in order to prevent as much [as] possible the sale of the English edition; and never place it in their windows or on their shop board." He therefore counseled Boswell "to employ some person here" to place an advertisement for the London edition through the Dublin bookseller to whom the book was consigned by the trades' "chief factor," who was none other than George Robinson (Baker, 1986, p. 420). But I have been unable to locate such an advertisement in the Dublin newspapers, and there is no evidence that Boswell took any further action that would affect the sale of his quarto edition in Ireland.

What Boswell called the "Country Sale" mainly involved English towns outside the metropolis. Table 2 records that 96 sets had been sold to "Dublin and Country" as of 4 April 1792. Thanks to Boswell's daily tabulation of such sales, which continued about one month longer, to 10 May 1792, it is possible to break down this figure, which had by then increased to 99. As Table 3 shows, copies of the *Life* were sent to booksellers in twelve English towns by 10 May, usually in very small numbers. Two towns stand out: Oxford, where Johnson had studied and was well connected (24 copies), and York (26 copies). The combined purchases made by booksellers in York and Oxford were about equal to the number of sets that Dilly sent to Edinburgh for Scottish sales. In all, booksellers in the twelve English "country" towns to which sales were made bought 78 copies by 10 May 1792, and 3 more sets went to Europe: 2 to Rotterdam and 1 to Paris. Unfortunately, Boswell did not record the names of these booksellers outside London.

Boswell's surviving sales records for the first edition are incomplete and sometimes confusing. Different segments of the sale were tabulated on different dates, and no sales figures of any kind exist after 13 June 1792, though the wholesale stock would not be exhausted until the following November. Nevertheless, the information that Boswell preserved is remarkable. Fully 1,603, or 95 percent, of the 1,689 copies made available for wholesale distribution by Boswell and Dilly can be accounted for by 13 June 1792: 1,401 (87.4 percent) to the London book trade (other than Dilly himself); 99 (6.2 percent) to booksellers in "country" towns (78 of them to Oxford, York, and other English towns, 18 to Dublin, and 3 to Rotterdam and Paris); 52 (3.2 percent) to booksellers in Edinburgh; and 51 (3.2 percent) to individual retail purchasers at

Table 3 "Country Sale" of the First Edition
(through 10 May 1792)

Place of Purchase	Sets Purchased
Dublin	18
York	26
Oxford	24
Bath	5
Bristol	5
Eton	4
Blandford	3
Norwich	3
Winchester	3
Worchester	2
Richmond	1
Tunbridge Wells	1
Ware	1
Rotterdam	2
Paris	1
Total	99

Source: Beinecke Rare Book and Manuscript
Library, Yale University, A 61, "Country Sale"

Dilly's shop. These proportions probably did not change very much as Dilly sold off the last remaining sets between June and November 1792.

The dominance of the London booksellers does not mean that all the retail purchasers of the first edition were residents of metropolitan London. The ten-shilling differential between the wholesale and retail price of the first edition left room for other London booksellers besides Dilly to distribute copies to book-sellers elsewhere at a profit. George Robinson, commonly called "the king of booksellers" by his peers, was said to maintain at the end of the eighteenth century "the largest wholesale trade that was ever carried on by an individual" (John Nichols, quoted in Raven, 2007, p. 243), not only in Britain but "in Europe" (William West, quoted in Sher, 2006, p. 388). Compared to Robinson's family firm, Dilly's business was a small-time operation. It is therefore likely that many copies of the *Life* that Robinson purchased from Dilly were meant for wholesale distribution, and perhaps also retail sales, beyond London. But no record of such sales has survived.

On 6 March 1793, after proudly informing Andrew Erskine that "1689 sets have been sold," Boswell boasted that "many more would have gone off could they have been had" (Waingrow, 2001, p. 399). Possibly, but considering how long it took for the last few dozen sets to sell, a larger print run would probably have been unwise, just as it would have been ill-advised to sell the copyright to George Robinson in advance of publication. Publishing 1,750 copies at his own risk was the best option for Boswell to maximize his return in a timely manner.

5 Beyond the First Edition

Boswell's approach to revising the *Tour* and the *Life* for later editions was generally reactive: most significant revisions were made in response to comments and criticisms received from others. But the ways in which this approach played out in the second editions of these two books were very different. Notable revisions to the *Tour* were made in response to criticisms by Scots who believed they had been misrepresented and sometimes maligned. Several were angry, and two of them – Alexander Fraser Tytler (later Lord Woodhouselee) and Sir Alexander Macdonald of Sleat (Lord Macdonald in the Irish peerage) – threatened violence, giving rise in the latter instance to satirical tracts and a print showing Boswell cowering in fear of Macdonald's cudgel (Figure 20). There were also severe time pressures because, according to the Advertisement in the second edition of the *Tour*, the first edition sold out "in a few weeks," and the second edition was therefore needed immediately. By contrast, the second edition of the *Life* appeared more than two years after publication of the first edition, and the most significant revisions derived from communications from favorably disposed friends and readers offering helpful comments, corrections, and new material. Boswell's method of revision remained reactive, but it was casual and additive rather than, as in the *Tour*, intense and defensive.

A second characteristic of Boswell's approach to preparing later editions (also evident in the first edition of the *Life*) was the practice of printing before the text was complete. As a result, if text to be revised had already been printed, problems ensued. While preparing the second edition of the *Tour*, for example, Boswell was unable to revise one passage because Malone informed him that it had just been printed (Baker, 1986, p. 266). By good fortune, the controversial passages concerning Tytler had not yet been printed because they occurred toward the end of the book. Softening the account of Macdonald was handled with a cancel leaf at pages 167–68, while the objections of another Scot, Thomas Blacklock, were addressed in an appendix (Sher, 2022, pp. 66–73, 348). These alterations did not detract from the coherence and appearance of

Figure 20 Thomas Rowlandson's *Picturesque Beauties of Boswell* (1786) satirized Boswell and Johnson's Scottish tour in a series of twenty prints. This one, titled "Revising for the Second Edition," quotes the second edition of Boswell's *Tour* on softening "a few observations . . . which might be considered as passing the bounds of a strict decorum," followed by a blistering couplet from a recent pamphlet by the satirist Peter Pindar (John Wolcot) (Pindar, 1786): "Let Lord McDonald threat thy breech to kick, / And o'er thy shrinking shoulders shake his stick." Beinecke Rare Book and Manuscript Library, Yale University

the second edition of the *Tour*. When Boswell worked on the second edition of the *Life of Johnson*, however, his casual, reactive, additive method of revision and his practice of printing before the revisions were complete, coupled with personal issues, caused serious delays and made a shambles of the book.

5.1 The Muddled Second Edition

On 3 May 1792 James Beattie sent Boswell a letter praising his "great work" but politely objecting to the words "He sunk upon us that he was married" in one of Johnson's comments about Beattie on 21 March 1772. Boswell inserted

Beattie's letter into a footnote near the end of the first volume in the second edition, along with a comment denying that the phrase "sunk upon us" was in any sense insulting. The same footnote explained why Beattie's letter did not appear at the place in the text where Johnson used the phrase "sunk upon us": "The first and second volumes of this edition having, in order to supply the publick demand speedily, been put to press at the same time, the passage to which the following letter from my friend Dr. Beattie alludes ... was printed off before his letter reached me" (Boswell, 1793, 1:601–2 n. 1). The proper place for Beattie's letter in the second edition was at the beginning of the second volume (2:3–4), but as those pages had already been printed, Boswell inserted it at the end of the first volume. Beattie's objection therefore appeared in the volume preceding the one that contained Johnson's objectionable words.

The "sunk upon us" episode epitomizes Boswell's predicament as he prepared the second edition of the *Life*. Simultaneous printing of the first two volumes – a variant of the process known to bibliographers as "concurrent production" (Gaskell, 1995, pp. 164–68) – began in late winter or early spring 1792 "in order to supply the publick demand speedily," as Boswell put it, and by 24 October the printing of those volumes and part of the third was complete (Waingrow, 2001, pp. 368, 381). An anonymous correspondent declared on 10 December that "the Public have a very strong Claim to an 8vo [i.e., octavo] Edition of your Work – Which it should be your Business to expedite as soon as possible" (p. 390). On 26 February 1793 Boswell informed Dr. William Maxwell in Ireland that "I shall soon have a second edition published here with corrections and considerable additions." His letter to Andrew Erskine on 6 March stated that it "will come forth early in April" (p. 399). In May he sent the printer a new Advertisement for the front matter of the first volume. Yet the octavo second edition was not published until 17 July 1793 – more than fifteen months after printing had begun and approximately eight months after Dilly sold off the first edition.

In addition to heavy drinking, depression, and difficulty focusing on the job at hand, the reactive, additive method of revision Boswell adopted was chiefly to blame for the delay because it was at cross-purposes with his aggressive printing policy: early, concurrent printing of the first two volumes was meant to speed up the production process, but incessant revisions, especially additions, had the opposite effect. Although Boswell made revisions of his own, mostly by modifying and expanding footnotes, much valuable new material was provided by members of his support network, including Langton, Nichols, Reed, Malone, and Reynolds before his death. Friendly letters containing useful comments, criticisms, and documents were received from individuals who had helped with the first edition, such as Edmund Hector (9 August 1791) and Maxwell (who sent "4 Folio sides of Johnsoniana" on 4 May 1793), as well as from several correspondents whom Boswell had not previously known, including Rev. Ralph Churton (9 March 1792), Rev. William Agutter (17 October 1792), and Rev. James Abercrombie of Philadelphia (25 January 1792) (Waingrow, 2001, pp. 339, 357–60, 362–66, 381, 408). Boswell incorporated the new material into his revised text as best he could. Sometimes he got lucky regarding placement, as when Reynolds found two letters from Johnson relating to the epitaph for Goldsmith (including the previously cited letter containing the words "show it to the Club"), which were inserted in their proper place at the beginning of the not-yet-printed Round Robin segment (Boswell, 1793, 2:448–49; *Life*, 3:81–82). But what was he to do if the text where the new material belonged had already been printed?

Three different solutions were devised. First, some new material was inserted into the book as close as possible to the place where it belonged. Boswell did this with the "sunk upon us" letter from Beattie, and he did it with two letters from Johnson to American correspondents, both dated 4 March 1773, that were received from Abercrombie. Those two letters should have appeared immediately after a letter of Johnson's dated 24 February 1773, but they had to be inserted sixty-eight pages later because the printing of the second volume had progressed too far (Boswell, 1793, 2:67, 135–38). The second solution occurred after Bennet Langton discovered a large stash of unpublished letters from Johnson. Since it was too late to put them in their proper places in the book, Boswell stuck them into the back of the second volume as a twenty-one-page appendix (though not so called). As he had done with the letter from Beattie, Boswell prefaced the new material from Langton with an apology for its placement: "*After the first two volumes of this Work were printed off, my worthy friend,* Mr. Langton ... *found the following valuable letters of* Dr. Johnson .... *Though it is impossible, in the present edition, to insert them in chronological order, I cannot withhold from my readers so great a satisfaction as the perusal of them must afford*" (Boswell, 1793, 2:613–34, quoting 613).

Still other material was added to the first volume of the second edition as front matter. After the dedication to Reynolds and the Advertisements to the first and second editions, Boswell inserted a disorganized 32-page section titled "Additions to Dr. Johnson's Life Recollected, and Received after the Second Edition Was Printed." It was followed by a new "Chronological Catalogue of the Prose Works of Samuel Johnson," which Boswell apparently added in response to a suggestion sent to him on 19 April 1793 by another well-meaning reader of the first edition, Rev. John Campbell of Kippen (Waingrow, 2001, pp. 403, 419). Next came a revised version of Tomlins's Alphabetical Table of Contents, a page with a new quotation from Shakespeare's *Henry VIII*, four pages of "Corrections" from all three volumes, and a page of "Additional Corrections." A reader opening the first volume of the second edition would be confronted, all told, with 86 pages of front matter in a chaotic jumble, with two different roman numeral page-numbering systems that were not always correct within themselves or in sync with each other. As late as 7 June 1793 the *Diary, or Woodfall's Register* printed a news item – almost certainly by Boswell – declaring that "Mr. Boswell is himself employed at present in making additions to his very amusing life of the great British Moralist."

Did Malone, a fastidious editor, approve of the muddled second edition of the *Life of Johnson*? Evidence is lacking that Boswell and Malone met as frequently to edit or revise the second edition as they had done formerly, and many errors entered the text because the proofs were not carefully corrected (Powell, 1928, pp. 54–59). There are also signs of growing tension between them. Boswell inserted into the second edition a long footnote from Malone questioning Johnson's remarks on Thomas Parnell's poem *The Hermit*, but he concluded the note by calling Malone's interpretation "much too recondite" (Boswell, 1793, 2:611 n. 6; *Life*, 3:393 n. 1). In an angry letter to Boswell of 13 May 1793, Malone vehemently denounced the additions Boswell made to their agreed-upon text of the Advertisement to the second edition (Baker, 1986, p. 423 & n. 1). At Malone's insistence, Boswell deleted one indiscreet paragraph involving the king. But Malone could not prevent his friend from retaining four other paragraphs – written after Boswell had "got into a higher flight of spirits" and become "less tractable," as Malone later told Forbes (Waingrow, 2001, p. 462) – which crowed about the "*spontaneous praise*" the *Life* had received from many eminent people and boasted that "*I have* Johnsonised *the land*" (*Life*, 1:13).

The angry letter from Malone of 13 May 1793 reveals that he encountered the offensive additions to the Advertisement only "by accident," as he happened to be in Baldwin's shop on the previous day. If Boswell did not show Malone his revised Advertisement before sending it to the printer, it is likely that he kept other revisions from him too, perhaps fearing Malone's disapproval. Besides the careless organization of the work, Malone might well have questioned some of the items in the "Additions to Dr. Johnson's Life Recollected" that were either self-serving (e.g., Johnson quoted from memory, with no date or context: "Boswell, (I think) I am easier with you than with almost any body") or so trivial that they became fodder for ridicule in the press (e.g., a long paragraph on Johnson's relationship with his cat, mocked in *The Oracle*, 24 July 1793; Werkmeister, 1963, pp. 50–51; Boswell, 1793, pp. *ix [i.e., *xiv], *xx–xxi; *Life*, 4:194, 197). Boswell also inserted into the "Additions" a previously misplaced document in which Johnson eloquently presents his case for the freedom of the slave Joseph Knight, followed by Boswell's bombastic tirade against "the wild and dangerous attempt" to abolish the slave trade (Boswell, 1793, pp. *ix [i.e., *xiv]–*xviii; Bonnell, 2012, pp. xvi, 146 & n. 6; *Life,* 3:200–5).

An advertisement for the second edition, "corrected, and considerably enlarged by additional Letters and interesting Anecdotes," appeared in the *London Chronicle* on 11 July 1793, setting 17 July as the date of publication and £1 4s. as the price in boards (Pottle, 1929, p. 168). The same advertisement ran in the London newspapers on 16 July, and subsequently, with the opening words changed to read "To-morrow, 17 July, will be published. . ." The price was only a few shillings more than the Dublin octavo, discouraging illegal importation of that edition into Britain. The advertisement notes a new engraving of Reynolds's portrait of Johnson by "[Joseph] Baker," a historical engraver in Islington (Maxted, 1977, p. 9). Although Pottle observed that Baker's engraving (Figure 21), dated 3 April 1793, is "distinctly inferior" to Heath's in the first edition (Pottle, 1929, p. 159), it achieved its purpose adequately and would continue to appear in several more editions. The engraved plates of the Round

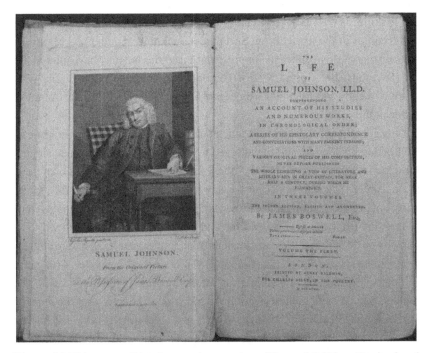

Figure 21 Title page of the three-volume octavo "Second Edition, Revised and Augmented" (1793), opposite Joseph Baker's frontispiece engraving of Johnson. Beinecke Rare Book and Manuscript Library, Yale University

Robin and of Johnson's signatures were adapted from the first edition, with the publication date of 10 April 1791 changed to 10 April 1793 – an easy alteration. As in the Dublin octavos, they were now folding plates because of their quarto size.

Although no impression or printing account has survived for the second edition, Boswell left behind cryptic manuscript notes about his expectations. Under the heading "Guess," he estimated that the second edition would use 128 sheets per set and would cost £662 for paper and print. These figures suggest a print run of 1,250 copies for three thick octavo volumes, with 1,500 as a less likely possibility. Boswell estimated an expense of £25 for the "Plates" – far less than the cost of the engravings for the first edition – and £23 for "Adverts. &c." (Yale, A 63), for a total cost of £710. On separate pages he tried to compute his income from the edition based on a wholesale price of seventeen shillings per set and Dilly's 7½ percent commission, but his calculations are difficult to follow. He gave away at least 32 presentation copies, in addition to some copies that he must have taken for his own use. Besides Malone, Langton, Reed, Courtenay, Tomlins, Plymsell, and Charles Baldwin from among those who had assisted with the first edition, presentation copies were awarded to several individuals who had supplied new material or corrections to the second edition, including Churton, Campbell, Abercrombie, and Erskine, as well as several family members who had not received presentation copies of the first edition. Still others, including Agutter and Maxwell, were on one of Boswell's lists for presentation copies but may have missed the cut (Seymour, 2016, pp. 424–28). The only woman outside the family who received a copy was Reynolds's niece and heiress Mary Palmer, now Countess of Inchiquin.

Dilly sold the second edition in much the same way as the first: with a sale to the London book trade, additional sales to booksellers elsewhere, and "single" sales to individual customers at his shop – all recorded in Boswell's own hand (Yale, A 62). The sale began on the day of publication, 17 July 1793, when thirty-six London firms purchased a total of 311 copies. Thirty more copies were sold to five firms the next day. At the end of the first week, Boswell wrote to Langton on 24 July that "Above 400 of the new Johnsonian Volumes are already sold. WONDERFUL MAN!" (Fifer, 1976, p. 387). The actual figure was 410, when 31 "country" sales and 17 "single" sales are combined with 362 sales to the London trade. On 22 August he told Malone, again correctly, that the number sold exceeded 500 (Baker, 1986, p. 426). It was a good start. Table 4 identifies the thirty-one London booksellers who purchased 12 or more copies during the eleven months in which Boswell recorded sales. The "Robinsons" were as usual well out in front, and most of the other booksellers whose names appear in Table 4 were also among those listed

Table 4 The Top Purchasers of the Second Edition (through 13 June 1794)

Bookseller or Firm	Location	Sets Purchased
"Robinsons" (George Robinson I and family)	Paternoster Row	79
David Ogilvie (Ogilvy)	Holborn	48
Henry Lasher Gardner	Strand	46
"Rivingtons" (Francis Rivington I and family)	St. Paul's Churchyard	38
William Richardson	Cornhill	30
James Lackington	Chiswell Street	27
Thomas Evans	Paternoster Row	24
Bedwell Law	Ave Maria Lane	24
Thomas Longman	Paternoster Row	24
Thomas Vernor	Birchin Lane (Cornhill)	24
White and Son (Benjamin II and John)	Fleet Street	24
Robert Faulder	New Bond Street	22
Joseph Bell	Oxford Street	18
Thomas Hookham	New Bond Street	18
William Otridge	Strand	18
John Payne	Paternoster Row	18
(James) Scatcherd & (J.) Whitaker	Ave Maria Lane	18
John Sewell	Cornhill	18
John Walter	Charing Cross	18
George Wilkie	St. Paul's Churchyard	18
Robert Baldwin	Paternoster Row	12
William Brown	Strand	12
Thomas Cadell Sr. (transitioning to Cadell & Davies from 1793)	Strand	12
John Debrett	Piccadilly	12
John Deighton	High Holborn	12
James Edwards	Pall Mall	12
Thomas and John Egerton	Charing Cross	12
Joseph Johnson	St. Paul's Churchyard	12
James Nunn	Great Queen Street	12
James Robson	New Bond Street	12
Henry Delahoy Symonds	Paternoster Row	12
SUBTOTAL		686
15 others with 10 or fewer purchases		84
TOTAL		**770**

in Table 1. In total, forty-six different firms purchased 770 copies. "Mrs. Harlow," who took 6 copies, was again the only woman to participate in the trade sale.

By the time Boswell stopped keeping records of the "single" sales on 9 April 1794, 34 copies of the second edition had been sold to retail customers in Dilly's bookshop. His record of "country" sales, extending to 10 May 1794, lists 49 purchases. This time he identified the purchasing booksellers in addition to their towns. William Stanes in Chelmsford purchased 11 copies, followed by "Croke" in Oxford (Joshua Cooke?) with 10, John Todd in York with 9, Christopher Berry III in Norwich with 8, William Tesseyman in York with 4, and Joseph Lloyd in Bristol with 1. Boswell included Dublin in the "country" sales of the second edition, but the only Dublin sale occurred when John Archer bought 6 copies on 22 July 1793. No sales to Edinburgh are listed, though it is likely that some copies were sent there that Boswell did not record. From the total sales he did record, we know that at least 853 copies of the octavo second edition had been unloaded by mid-June 1794: 770 (or just over 90 percent) to the London trade exclusive of Dilly, 49 to "country" towns, including Dublin, and 34 to individuals who purchased their copies from Dilly's shop at the retail price.

These sales figures were encouraging at first but, perhaps because the second edition was such a careless production, they tailed off over time. During this period, Dilly kept up Boswell's spirits by telling him that "the sale of my Book was going on as might be expected," as Boswell wrote in his journal entry for 11 January 1794. On 29 January, however, Boswell recorded that he "Sat a while at Dilly's, and found that the sale of my Life of Dr. Johnson had stagnated for some time, which discouraged me." Nevertheless, on 17 March he told his son Alexander that although the "second edition of Dr. Johnson's *Life* has sold not so rapidly as the first," more than 800 copies had been disposed of, and "I doubt not but the whole impression will *move* (as the Booksellers say) before this time twelvemonth" (quoted in Waingrow, 2001, p. lxix). This prediction would turn out to be far from the mark, and a third edition would not be required for several more years.

5.2 Reconfiguring the Second Edition

An advertisement for the second edition in the *London Chronicle* on 14 September 1793 (Figure 22) contains new information on two different subjects. First, in continuing to hawk the third edition of the *Tour* – with the map inserted in 1791 to boost sagging sales – this advertisement introduces a new concept: "N. B. This volume, with the three now published, form the complete Life of Dr. Johnson by Mr. Boswell, who has referred to it as a distinct portion." Although the phrasing is awkward, the meaning is clear: Boswell was declaring that the expanded three

This Day was publiſhed,
In Three large Vols. 8vo. Price 1l. 4s. in boards,
THE LIFE of SAMUEL JOHNSON, LL.D.
By JAMES BOSWELL, Eſq.

The Second Edition, corrected, and conſiderably enlarged by additional Letters and intereſting Anecdot·s.

The whole exhibiting a View of Literature and Literary Men in Great Britain for near half a Century.

Illuſtrated with an engraved Portrait of Dr. Johnſon, by Baker, after his firſt Picture by Sir Joſhua Reynolds, and Fac-ſimilies of his Hand-writing, and of that of various eminent Men of his Time.

. Printed for Charles Dilly, in the Poultry.

☞ .While no pains have been ſpared to improve this Work, the CORRECTIONS and ADDITIONS are printed ſeparately in Quarto, for the accommodation of the Purchaſers of the Firſt Edition; and may now be had of Mr. Dilly, price 2s. 6d.

Of whom alſo may be had,

. Mr. Boſwell's Journal of a Tour to the Hebrides with Dr. Johnſon, in one volume octavo, the third edition, illuſtrated with a map deſcribing the route of the travellers.

N. B. This volume, with the three now publiſhed, form the complete Life of Dr. Johnſon by Mr. Boſwell, who has referred to it as a diſtinct portion.

Figure 22 Advertisement for the second edition, *London Chronicle*, 14 September 1793. Burney Newspapers Collection

volumes of the second edition of the *Life* and the one-volume third edition of the *Tour* – octavos of comparable height and thickness – were meant to comprise a "complete" biography of Johnson. This claim was buttressed in another advertisement for the second edition, which referred to the *Tour* (now priced at 7s.), with emphasis, "*as a separate Portion* of the Life of that great Man, and which, with these Volumes, completes it" (*Times*, 13 December 1793). Were these statements merely an advertising ploy? If so, it did not work. On 24 August 1796 Dilly told Forbes that "The demand for the Tour to the Highlands is decreasing and I believe there hath not been a Dozen Copies sold thro' the present Year – and the Books in hand 430 cannot be sold but as remainders" – to be marked down to just one shilling. He added that "many Books when the demand is over will produce no more than Waste Paper" (quoted in McGowan, 1996, p. 142). If, however, the statements in these advertisements are taken at face value, they may be said to represent Boswell's final view of the *Tour* and the *Life* as constituting a single, integrated biographical work.

The *London Chronicle* advertisement on 14 September 1793 also contains new information about *The Principal Corrections and Additions to the First Edition of Mr. Boswell's Life of Dr. Johnson.* The last sentence of the *London Chronicle* advertisement for the second edition of the *Life* on 11 July had stated that "the Corrections and Additions are printed separately in Quarto, for the accommodation of the Purchasers of the First Edition," who could have it bound at the end of the second volume. Boswell's wording fostered a mistaken belief that "The *Corrections and Additions* appeared simultaneously with the second edition" (Pottle, 1929, p. 214) and was "distributed free to owners of the first edition" (Brady, 1984, p. 478). However, the advertisement on 14 September adds these words after the reference to this work: "and may now be had of Mr. Dilly, price 2s. 6d." This statement, along with the same price printed on the title page itself and in a subsequent advertisement (*Times*, 13 December 1793), establishes that the *Principal Corrections and Additions* was published two months after the second edition of the *Life* and had to be purchased separately by owners of the first edition. Letters to Barnard and Blair on 16 August and 3 November 1792 show that Boswell originally intended to "give" it to owners of the first edition (Fifer, 1976, p. 373; Yale, L 62.2, copy), but he changed his mind at some point, presumably because of the expense. He did, however, send presentation copies to some people who had received presentation copies of the first edition (e.g., Fifer, 1976, pp. 392–93; Seymour, 2016, p. 422).

Bearing the usual Dilly-Baldwin imprint, the *Principal Corrections and Additions* is a thin (Figure 3), closely printed volume of 42 pages of text (37 of corrections and additions, followed by 5 pages containing the "Chronological Catalogue" of Johnson's prose works), with Boswell's name printed at the end to signify its authenticity. Boswell provided the locations in the first edition where the revisions and additions should go, rather than the places where they appear in the second edition. He also corrected some errors in the second edition that were brought to his attention by Langton (Fifer, 1976, pp. 387–92) and others. A journal entry on 6 August 1793 states that printing this work was then his "only *business*," and when dining at Baldwin's seven days later he commented on how "comfortable" he felt "to have such a hospitable table at my printer's, where there is good cheer and hearty welcome." The editing was not done carefully, however, as shown by the handwritten corrections in surviving copies and other errors, such as the inadvertent omission on page 19 of a sentence added in the second edition to the Round Robin footnote shown in Figure 16b, giving Johnson's reaction to Burke: "'I should have thought Mund Burke would have had more sense'" (Boswell, 1793, 2:451 n. 7; *Life*, 3:84 n. 2). As no records have survived about the *Principal Corrections and Additions*, it is not known how many copies were printed or sold, or whether Boswell was able to recoup his expenses.

On 3 October 1793, shortly after the appearance of the *Principal Corrections and Additions* and less than a year after Boswell's "feast" to celebrate the first edition of the *Life*, Boswell wrote in his journal that Henry Baldwin "kindly gave an entertainment . . . an excellent City dinner" to celebrate the second edition. The guests were drawn from Boswell's support network – Dilly, Malone, Nichols, Tomlins, Alexander Chalmers, and David Boswell – as well as Alderman (and former Lord Mayor) Richard Clark, "a gentleman for whom [Johnson] deservedly entertained a great regard" (*Life*, 4:258). As at the first celebration, Boswell "did my part as well as I could; but my gloom was heavy." A few days earlier (24–26 September) he had written in his journal of being "in a woeful state of depression in every respect" as he came to grips with the fact that he no longer had prospects for a career or a meaningful life in London or Scotland. He struggled with such thoughts for much of the last year and a half of his life, until his death from a urinary tract ailment on 19 May 1795, at the age of fifty-four.

5.3 Profiting from the *Life*

How much did Boswell earn from the two editions of the *Life of Johnson* that appeared during his lifetime? Joseph Farington caused much confusion by leaving two different accounts in his diary, one from 13 July 1795, stating that Boswell earned £1,550 from the quarto first edition, "to be made up £2000 on acct. of the Octavo [second] edition," and the other from 31 January 1805, claiming that "Boswell in his life time made about £2500 by this work" (Farington, 1978–84, 2:366, 7:2507). Both accounts are inflated. The profit from the octavo second edition would not have reached £450 (and therefore £2,000 for the first and second editions combined) even if all the copies had been sold while Boswell was alive. And that did not happen. The 853 copies that Dilly sold by mid-June 1794 would have brought Boswell, in his capacity as publisher, £725 in gross revenue at the wholesale price of seventeen shillings per set – less than his estimated expenses of £710, when Dilly's commission was added. Early in 1795 Dilly paid Boswell £132 8s. on the sale of 200 copies (in addition to £7 2s. previously advanced to him), and he received an additional £27 18s. on the sale of 40 more copies in early spring 1795. On both these occasions, Boswell's payments were calculated at what Dilly termed the "Sale Price" of 15s. 6d. per three-volume set rather than the wholesale price of 17s. (Yale, A 64). These transactions appear to represent partial payments that enabled Boswell to obtain some badly needed income as it became clear that the second edition was not going to sell out quickly.

Thus, Boswell's lifetime profits from the *Life of Johnson* appear to have been £1,723 6s. 2d. (£1,555 18s. 2d. from the first edition and £167 8s. from the second). Although less than Farington thought, this was still a great deal of money, and after Boswell's death further profits stood to be made because the estate still owned the copyright and the remaining stock of the second edition. On 14 October 1795 – five months after Boswell's death and scarcely two weeks after the death from consumption of the eldest Boswell child, Veronica – Sir William Forbes, on behalf of Boswell's "younger children" (i.e., all the surviving children except the heir, Alexander, regardless of their ages; Pottle, 1982, p. 10 n. 2), agreed to sell to Dilly all the unsold copies of the second edition at a reduced price of twelve shillings each (Fettercairn Papers, box 87, draft). Although the number of unsold copies is not known, this transaction would have produced £60 per 100 unsold copies for Boswell's "younger children."

6 *Life* after Boswell

After Boswell died, the *Life of Johnson* passed into the hands of his support network. Although the second edition had been disappointing, demand for the book continued. The task of producing a third edition fell chiefly to three familiar figures: Charles Dilly, who would be in charge of overseeing all aspects of the publication and sales, including printing by the firm now run unofficially – and during the first decade of the new century officially – by Henry Baldwin's son Charles; Edmond Malone, to whom Boswell had left "all my Collection of Papers and Letters and Memorandums for writing the Life of Dr. Johnson" in a codicil to his will (quoted in Pottle, 1982, p. 9); and Sir William Forbes, in his dual capacity as the executor of Boswell's estate and the co-guardian, with David Boswell, of Boswell's "younger children," to whom Boswell had bequeathed the copyright to the *Life* (Sher, 2022, p. 315). An advertisement for the third edition appeared in the Baldwins' *St. James's Chronicle* on 5 April 1798, with the heading "*In the Press, and speedily will be published / With the last Corrections of the Authour*" (Figure 23). Yet at this time the three principals had neither reached agreement about the text of the third edition nor begun preparing it for the press. Hence the advertisement contains no information about the edition or its price and is largely devoted to two other works for sale at Dilly's bookshop: the third edition of the *Tour* with the map added in 1791 – advertised for six shillings in boards despite Dilly's earlier plan to remainder it for a shilling – and another one-volume, six-shilling octavo in boards: the book for which Boswell had granted approval to Dilly and Thomas Wright in July 1791, *Dr. Johnson's Table-Talk*, "just published."

Surviving correspondence between Dilly and Forbes (Fettercairn Papers, box 87) and between Forbes and Malone (Waingrow, 2001, pp. 461–64) from spring and summer 1798 reveals the nature of their differences. Dilly wanted to move quickly so that the printing could take place that summer, "when Book's of magnitude are commonly Printed" (letter to Forbes, 28 June). Forbes's chief concern, however, was to delete some of Boswell's more hurtful expressions regarding living individuals, such as Thomas Percy (p. 461). On 12 July Dilly agreed that "the Work requires a little pruning" and, under the impression that Malone thought so too, he asked Forbes to send him any "exceptionable passages."

In the Prefs, and fpeedily will be publifhed,
With the laft Corrections of the Authour,
The THIRD EDITION, of
THE LIFE of SAMUEL JOHNSON, LL. D.
Comprehending an Account of his Studies and numerous
Works; and exhibiting a View of Literature and Literary Men
for nearly Half a Century, during which he flourifhed.
By JAMES BOSWELL, Efq.
London : Printed for C. Dilly, in the Poultry.
Of whom may be had, juft publifhed,
In One Volume, Octavo, Price 6s. in Boards,
Dr. JOHNSON's TABLE-TALK: containing APHO-
RISMS on LITERATURE, LIFE, and MANNERS; with
Anecdotes of diftinguifhed Perfons: felected and arranged from
Mr. Bofwell's Life of Johnfon.
Alfo, The Third Edition, in 8vo. Price 6s. in Boards,
The JOURNAL of a TOUR to the HEBRIDES, with Dr.
JOHNSON. By JAMES BOSWELL, Efq. Containing a
Series of his Converfation, Literary Anecdotes, and Opinions of
Men and Books. To which is prefixed, A Map of the Tour
through Scotland and the Hebrides.

Figure 23 Advertisement for the third edition of the *Life*, with *Dr. Johnson's Table-Talk* and the slow-selling third edition of the *Tour*, in the *St. James's Chronicle*, 5 April 1798. Burney Newspapers Collection

In a letter to Forbes of 5 July, however, Malone was adamant that "the work of an author is sacred," and not a single word of Boswell's text should be deleted or altered – including the passages in the Advertisement to the second edition that he considered "very faulty" (p. 462). Reassured by Malone that the objectionable expressions had been removed in the second edition, and that Boswell and Percy had reconciled before Boswell's death (p. 463), Forbes told Dilly on 20 July that "I now fully agree to your proposal for printing a new edition in Octavo of Mr. Boswell's life of Johnson, *as it now stands*" (draft; emphasis added). Dilly had informed him in his letter of 12 July that "The Interleaved Copy which Young Boswell [James, then aged twenty] has deliverd to his Uncle [David Boswell] contains a few corrections of the Author only – and this Set perhaps sh[oul]d be the one to be Printed from." Believing that this corrected copy resolved the issue, Forbes authorized Dilly to "begin to print the Book whenever you please."

Malone understood that the matter was not that simple. The third edition of the *Life* would not appear until 18 May 1799 – more than thirteen months after the advertisement asserting that it was "In the Press" and would be published "speedily." The "Advertisement to the Third Edition" prefixed to the first volume, signed by Malone and dated 8 April 1799, states that Boswell had been obliged to introduce into his second edition as "ADDENDA" the "valuable letters, and other curious matter" which had been communicated to him "too late to be arranged in that chronological order which he had endeavoured uniformly to observe in his work." These items "have been distributed in their proper places." Malone comments further that "In revising his volumes for a new edition," Boswell "had pointed out where some of these materials should be inserted." But the word "some" indicates that Malone himself had to decide where an undetermined portion of the new materials should go. "All the Notes that he had written in the margin of the copy which he had in part revised, are here faithfully preserved," he adds (*Life*, 1:14–15). Unfortunately, Boswell's annotated copy of the *Life* cited by Malone – undoubtedly the "Interleaved Copy" that Dilly mentions in his letter to Forbes of 12 July 1798 – has never been found, and Boswell left behind no other evidence of work on the third edition. Yet excepting a sizeable number of typographical errors (a problem going forward, as L. F. Powell notes in *Life*, 1: v–vi) and a cumbersome appendix to volume four (pp. 461–66), the third edition is a generally coherent and neatly organized book containing Boswell's last known revisions and Malone's expert editing, and that is why it is usually considered the standard edition today (Boswell, 1998; Boswell, 2008). Among other things, the third edition transformed the Alphabetical Table of Contents in the first and second editions into a proper – and expanded – index at the end of the work. Malone also added many new footnotes by himself and others, including a refutation of Boswell's "much too recondite" criticism in the second edition (Boswell, 1799, 3:419). These revisions took time to prepare.

An advertisement in the *Morning Chronicle* on 18 May 1799 announced publication that day of the "revised and augmented" third edition in four octavo volumes. At £1 8s. in boards, the price was four shillings more than the second edition for a work that was superior in organization and appearance – printed on fine paper with better type in four slender volumes rather than three thick ones (Pottle, 1929, pp. 169–70). The advertisement devoted as much space to the troublesome third edition of the *Tour* as to the third edition of the *Life*, as Dilly kept trying to unload the large stock of the older book.

Figure 24 reproduces the impression account for the third edition of the *Life*, dated 28 June 1800, which Dilly sent to Forbes. The print run was 1,250 copies, and the base costs and wholesale price were similar to Boswell's projections for the second edition: Boswell had estimated for the second edition 128 sheets of paper per set, a total cost for paper and print of £662, and a wholesale price of seventeen shillings; the third edition used 123½ sheets of fine wove demy paper per set, cost £611 11s. 4d. for paper and print, and had a wholesale price of eighteen shillings. The cost of the paper (£391 16s. 4d.) was almost twice as much as the cost of Baldwin's charges for printing (£219 15s., including corrections and index).

Dilly also records £44 12s. in incidental charges ("Incidents") for the third edition. The largest of these Incidents was £21 paid "To the Editor Mr. Tomlins for correcting new Index" (in addition to the separate charge of £4 10s. for printing it). That fee may have covered more than revising the index, because Tomlins is identified as "the Editor," and Dilly told Forbes on 12 July 1798 that "the Gentleman who corrected the Proof Sheets for Mr. Boswell – or at least Assisted will do the same in the one about to be printed" (Fettercairn Papers, box 87). Tomlins's involvement with the second and third editions raises the prospect that other familiar figures from the Baldwin print shop may have continued to work with Tomlins, Malone, and Charles Baldwin on later editions of the *Life*.

Another of the Incidents is a charge of £1 8s. for binding (i.e., boarding) eleven sets of "presents" – meaning the gift copies for Malone, Forbes, David Boswell, Boswell's two sons, and several others who had contributed new notes and other materials to the third edition. A presentation copy also went to "the Editor of the B: Critic," Malone's friend Robert Nares, editor of the Tory monthly *The British Critic*, which had explicitly looked forward to the third edition of the *Life* in its February 1794 combined review of the second edition and the *Principal Corrections and Additions*. The Incidents also contain a charge of £14 2s. for the engravings, including four guineas to Joseph Baker for repairing the plate of his frontispiece portrait of Johnson from the second edition. The expenditure for engravings was relatively low because they had only to be repaired and then printed off from the three existing plates by the copperplate engraver hired for that purpose, Thomas Ross of Cow Lane in Snow Hill (Maxted, 1977, p. 194). Finally, there is a charge of £8 2s. for "Sundry Adv[er]t[isement]s: prior to & since the Publication." To these charges for Incidents Dilly adds £28 10s. that I cannot explain: £17 14s. as an additional charge of 5 percent on sales to the trade and £10 16s. for twelve sets lost on account of "the Failure of Earley Hamets."

The publishing terms for the third edition were unlike those for the two editions that Boswell had published at his own risk. Instead of taking only a 7½ percent commission on wholesale income, Dilly shared both the expenses and the profits equally with Boswell's estate, as he often did with his other publications. In a letter to Dilly of 3 December 1799, Forbes calls this a "very fair" arrangement (Fettercairn Papers, box 90, draft). If the entire third edition had been sold off, the gross income would have been approximately £1,115, based on 1,239 sets (1,250 minus 11 "presents") sold at the wholesale price of eighteen shillings. Subtracting from this amount the expenses of paper and print, the Incidents, and the additional charges of £28 10s. would have yielded a net profit of approximately £431, to be divided equally between Dilly and the author's estate. Forbes would then have received £215 10s. for distribution to Boswell's three surviving "younger children," Euphemia, James, and Elizabeth. But this scenario did not actually occur. Dilly's impression account reveals that only 394 sets of the third edition were "sold to the Trade" at the wholesale price of eighteen shillings during the first thirteen months after publication, and no other sales are mentioned. With so many copies unsold, and James and Euphemia hard-pressed for funds as they tried to make their way in London with

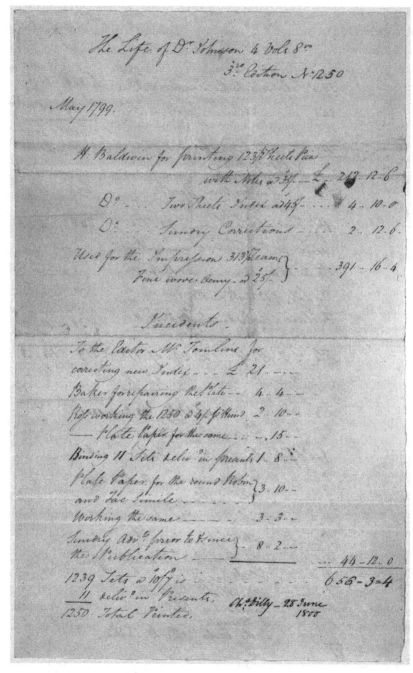

Figure 24a The first page of Dilly's impression account for the 1799 third edition, showing the charges for the printing, paper, and "Incidents." National Library of Scotland, Fettercairn Papers, Acc. 4796, box 90, folder 1

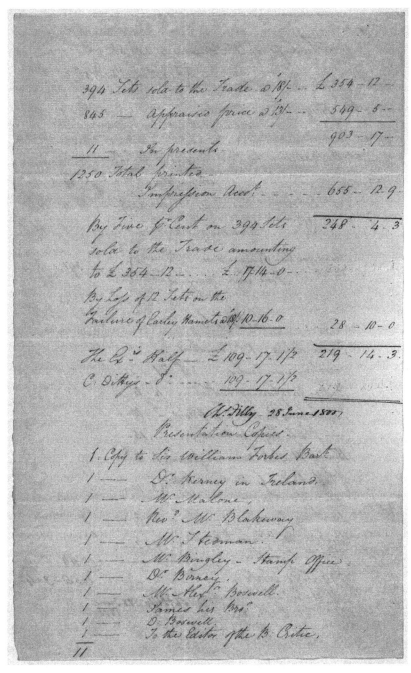

Figure 24b The second page of the impression account for the third edition, showing sales to the book trade at the wholesale price, sales of the unsold copies to Dilly at the "appraised price," the net profits divided equally between the Boswell estate and Dilly, and the 11 recipients of presentation copies. National Library of Scotland, Fettercairn Papers, Acc. 4796, box 90, folder 1

annuities of no more than £150 and £100, respectively (Farington, 1978–84, 2:465, 5:1633; Sher, 2022, p. 311), Forbes sold the remaining stock to Dilly for the "appraised price" of just thirteen shillings per copy. The total profit came to only £219 14s. 3d., and "The Ex[ecuto]r[']s Half" was £109 17s. ½d. – or less than £37 each for Euphemia, James, and Elizabeth. As in the case of the second edition, a bargain was struck with Dilly to obtain a smaller amount of income more quickly.

In the letter of 14 October 1795 accepting Dilly's offer to purchase the remaining stock of the second edition of the *Life* at a reduced price, Forbes had also raised the issue of selling the copyright: "If you shall be inclined to treat for the Copyright of the Book, I shall be glad to hear what you think it may be worth to you" (Fettercairn Papers, box 87, draft). Dilly had no interest in Forbes's offer. During the second half of the 1790s he was winding down his business with a view toward retirement, which took place in 1801. The slow initial sales of the third edition probably stemmed in part from Dilly's declining involvement in business affairs. On 8 May 1802 young James Boswell, still seriously short of funds, told Forbes about his attempts to sell the copyright in London: "I applied to [Joseph] Mawman (Mr. Dilly's Successor) about the life & to my astonishment he only offerd one hundred pounds. However when Mr. Dilly returns to Town I shall with his assistance apply to other book<sellers> & try if we cannot make a more rational barg<ain>." The first of two letters to Forbes from Boswell's daughter Euphemia, undated but probably from late 1802 or early 1803, explained that another bookseller had offered James £300, with the added incentive that £200 of it would be paid "immediately." Concerned about the expiration of the copyright in 1805, Euphemia and James would accept that offer, which turned out to be from Cadell & Davies – the premier London bookselling firm after the death of George Robinson in 1801. "Had I been but possessed of ready Cash," Euphemia added, "it should not have been sold, for such a poor sum" (Fettercairn Papers, box 88). Malone was consulted, and after Forbes, and presumably also David Boswell, gave their approval, the sale was concluded. Boswell's surviving "younger children" would receive the proceeds, but the Boswell family's financial interest in the *Life of Johnson* was severed forever.

On 31 January 1805 Joseph Farington wrote in his diary that Cadell & Davies's purchase of the copyright to the *Life* for £300 "has proved a very good bargain" (Farington, 1978–84, 7:2507). But why was it a very good bargain to purchase the copyright for that amount in 1803 if the copyright was due to expire fourteen years after publication, in the spring of 1805? Although Cadell & Davies published a fourth edition in four octavo volumes in early summer 1804, that edition alone probably did not generate much more profit than they had paid for the copyright. In one of her undated letters to Forbes, Euphemia had remarked that after the copyright expired, "any person can Print the Book." Why didn't this situation deter Cadell & Davies?

Cadell & Davies could employ a tactic that was not available to private copyright owners such as the Boswell children. To explain how "the booksellers of London" secured the publication rights to the works of the many poets in their 1779–81 compilation, for which Johnson wrote "Prefaces, biographical and critical," the *Life* cites "honorary copy right, which is still preserved among them by mutual compact, notwithstanding the decision of the House of Lords [in 1774] against the perpetuity of Literary Property" (*Life*, 3:370). According to this practice, the London booksellers agreed to honor each other's literary property, even if the term of statutory copyright had expired. Thomas Cadell Sr. had been among the most vociferous defenders of this policy (Sher, 1998, pp. 40–42; Sher, 2006, pp. 353–54), and Cadell & Davies continued the tradition. On 28 October 1814 James Boswell the younger applied this "rule among Booksellers" to the *Life of Johnson* specifically (Farington, 1978–84, 13:4601).

A second tactic used by the London booksellers was to revise and expand each new edition, so that the copyright clock would continually reset. The intent was to create the perception that later editions were superior because they contained important new material. The Strahans and Cadells employed this practice to sustain the popularity of some of their best-selling books, such as William Buchan's *Domestic Medicine* (Sher, 1999, pp. 54–55). With respect to the *Life of Johnson*, Boswell himself began this tradition in the second edition, which featured the phrase "Revised and Augmented" on the title page (the second and third editions of the *Tour* had used the less ambitious words "Revised and Corrected"). The advertisement for the second edition in the *Times* on 13 December 1793 announced that "this Edition is enriched with upwards of One Hundred and Fifty additional Pages." After the death of the author, the *Life* was expanded posthumously, without altering Boswell's text, by inserting new footnotes and by adding new pieces of correspondence. Pottle remarked that the fourth edition "began the practice . . . of enlarging the text with unpublished letters which had not been available to Boswell" (Pottle, 1929, p. 171). But he did not indicate that publishers encouraged this practice because of its implications for copyright extension. Of course, textual augmentation could also justify higher prices.

Revising and augmenting could not be done effectively by just anyone, however. After taking over the *Life of Johnson*, Cadell & Davies wisely retained key members of the editorial and printing team that had previously supported Boswell's book. Until his death in April 1812, Malone continued as the editor of the fourth (1804), fifth (1807), sixth (1811), and seventh (also 1811, in a smaller and cheaper five-volume duodecimo format) editions, and by extension also the eighth edition (1816), which like the seventh simply reproduced the text of the sixth edition, though it added a new version of the frontispiece engraving. All these editions display the phrase "Revised and Augmented" on their title pages, and the sixth edition earned respect for its editorial notes, new letters from Johnson, and systematic corrections by James Boswell the younger – though it also introduced some new typographical errors (*Life*, 1:vi). Then, after Davies's death in 1819, Cadell opened the publishing rights to more than a half dozen other London booksellers (including the firm of Henry Baldwin's nephew Robert Baldwin III), with whom he co-published one more edition, the ninth, in 1822. It was edited by another of Boswell's friends, and Malone's hand-picked successor, Alexander Chalmers, who continued the tradition of adding notes and corrections while not tampering with Boswell's words (Pottle, 1929, pp. 171–76).

Pottle noted that "all the editions of the *Life* from the first to the ninth inclusive (1791–1822)" were printed by "the house of Baldwin" (Pottle, 1929, p. 176) – very possibly still including compositors and correctors who had worked on earlier editions. From the fourth edition the *Life* benefited from its association with the Cadell & Davies bookselling empire, with its massive annual sales catalogues, hallowed location in the Strand, and extensive connections throughout and beyond Britain, far exceeding the reach of Dilly's relatively modest business. During the entire run of six consecutive Cadell/Baldwin editions, from 1804 to 1822, no other British bookseller dared to issue a rival edition of the *Life*, though the copyright of the first edition had expired in 1805. Such was the effect of "honorary copyright" and textual augmentation in the hands of a powerful publisher, along with the authority of editors and printers who had a claim to authenticity based on their ties to the author and the book. We can now see why Cadell & Davies's purchase of the copyright for £300 in 1803 was "a very good bargain" indeed.

The fate of the *Life of Johnson* in the quarter of a century or more following Boswell's death was a triumph of the Boswellian support network. The consequences can be seen in Thomas Babington Macaulay's famous review of John Wilson Croker's five-volume edition of the *Life* in the September 1831 issue of the *Edinburgh Review* (54:1–38). The review castigates Croker for making many errors and for bastardizing Boswell's book, and it brutalizes Boswell himself, for whom Macaulay had contempt (54:16–17). Yet, according to Macaulay, "The Life of Johnson is assuredly a great – a very great work"; it is "one of the best books in the world" (54:16–17), and "Boswell is the first of biographers. He has no second. He has distanced all his competitors so decidedly that it is not worth while to place them" (54:16). Macaulay wrongly assumed that the *Life* was a fixed and unchanging entity, when in fact it had undergone significant expansion in the four decades since its original appearance. He was correct, however, in maintaining that Croker had crossed a line by expurgating and altering portions of Boswell's text in a manner that Malone, Chalmers, and James Boswell the younger would never have tolerated. It was because Malone and the surviving remnant of the Boswellian publishing network fully appreciated Boswell's biographical genius that they took pains to remain true to his legacy. Although Macaulay despised Boswell, he could not deny his achievement as a biographer.

In 1791 James Boswell wrote and published the *Life of Johnson* in collaboration with Edmond Malone, Charles Dilly, Henry Baldwin, and other members of his support network. It was a huge success, but its future was not guaranteed. The muddled second edition demonstrated that publication at one's own risk could be problematic if an author-publisher was not functioning effectively. After Boswell died in 1795, his evolving support network not only kept his book alive but built it into a classic, acclaimed by the beginning of Victoria's reign as the greatest of all biographies.

7 Conclusion

What lessons can be learned from this study, and what kinds of questions does it raise for future scholarship? It should now be clear that Boswell's role in the making of the *Life of Johnson* was much greater than has traditionally been thought. As the author-publisher of a large and expensive book, Boswell risked not only his literary reputation but also his financial stability and even his mental health on his quest to erect a "literary monument" to his "illustrious friend." Fortunately for him, he did not undertake that quest alone. We have seen that his support network was large, loyal, and diverse, encompassing not only members of The Club, his "Gang," and his wider circle of friends but also individuals from the book and periodical trades and others who contributed in one way or another. Further research will be necessary to explore the implications of these findings for the study of Boswell and his intellectual and social milieu, as well as for his achievement as a biographer.

Another topic for further research concerns the effects of Boswell's publication and marketing decisions on readers' perceptions of Johnson. An exceptionally large print run of two thick quarto volumes on fine paper signaled that Johnson was a large and imposing figure of major importance. The frontispiece engraved from a portrait by Sir Joshua Reynolds displayed a dignified, contemplative scholar in his study – very different from the Reynolds portrait on the covers of the best modern editions of the *Life* (Boswell, 1998; Boswell, 2008), showing a severely near-sighted man whom Johnson himself derisively termed "*blinking Sam*" (Piozzi, 1786, p. 142; Folkenflik, 2014). The placement of the date and Johnson's age in the upper left-hand corner of every page, as shown in Figure 16b, reinforced the claim in the introduction to the *Life* that one of Boswell's central methodological principles was to examine "the chronological series of Johnson's life, which I trace as distinctly as I can, year by year" (*Life*,

1:29). Publicizing the letter to Chesterfield and the conversation with the king highlighted Boswell's conception of Johnson's character.

These observations may be seen as an extension of the revolution in bibliography precipitated by D. F. McKenzie's 1985 Panizzi Lectures, which asked – and famously answered in the affirmative – "whether or not the material forms of books [i.e., "typography and layout"] have an expressive function in conveying meaning" (McKenzie, 1999, p. 17, 25). There is now a rich literature on the varied ways that certain eighteenth-century writers of poetry and fiction engaged with their publishers to shape the appearance of their books (e.g., McKenzie, 2002, ch. 8; Barchas, 2003; Flint, 2011; Williams, 2021, esp. p. 4), as well as a comprehensive study of the significance of the standardization of the modern page owing to the decline in capitalization and italics (Wendorf, 2022). What does the story told here add to this body of scholarship? Put differently, how can Mackenzie's "sociology of texts" be transformed into a full-blown sociology of books?

Was Boswell's role in the making of the *Life of Johnson* unique? This question has no easy answer. On the one hand, it is difficult to imagine another author-publisher having anything quite like the vast number of intimate, dedicated, sometimes financially supportive relationships that Boswell had with his bookseller, his printer, and other members of his support network. On the other hand, some other late eighteenth-century author-publishers, such as Robert Henry, produced books on a scale as large or larger than the *Life of Johnson*, with bigger financial returns from their quarto volumes and from subsequent sales of the copyright. Even some octavos "Printed for the Author" or published by subscription attained high levels of sales and profits (e.g., Sher, 2006, ch. 3). Furthermore, it is not known how many other books were "Printed for the Author" even though that phrase does not appear in their imprints, or if other author-publishers participated as fully as Boswell in the publishing and marketing process. The subject is ripe for further investigation.

In all such studies, sources loom large. Unlike the startling discoveries of treasure troves of Boswell manuscripts at Malahide and Fettercairn, many of the main sources used in this work spent decades hiding in plain sight in eighteenth-century newspapers and periodicals and in manuscript collections in major libraries. These sources are unusually rich and abundant for the *Life of Johnson*, but it remains to be seen if they are unique. Much depends on diligently searching for unpublished as well as published correspondence, diaries, book trade records, newspaper advertisements and "news" items, pamphlets, and other relevant materials, and then asking questions that can yield useful information about the making of books.

References

Alexander, David (2021). *A Biographical Dictionary of British and Irish Engravers, 1714–1820*. New Haven, CT: Yale University Press.

Amory, Hugh & Hall, David D., eds. (2000). *A History of the Book in America. Volume 1: The Colonial Book in the Atlantic World*. Cambridge: Cambridge University Press.

Anecdote, Sir Andrew (pseud.) (1792). *A Collection of Interesting Biography. Containing, I. The Life of S. Johnson, LL.D. Abridged, Principally from Boswell's Celebrated Memoirs of the Doctor: II. The Life of Mr. Elwes (Abridged) by Captain Topham: III. The Life of Captain Cook, (Abridged) by Dr. Kippis*. Dublin: P. Wogan, P. Byrne. [reprint of 1791 London ed.]

Anon. [Stephen Jones?] (1798). *Dr. Johnson's Table-Talk: Containing Aphorisms of Literature, Life, and Manners; with Anecdotes of Distinguished Persons: Selected and Arranged from Mr. Boswell's Life of Johnson*. London: Dilly.

Baird, Ileana, ed. (2014). *Social Networks in the Long Eighteenth Century: Clubs, Literary Salons, Textual Coteries*. Newcastle upon Tyne: Cambridge Scholars.

Baker, Peter S., Copeland, Thomas W., Kahrl, George M., McClellan, Rachel & Osborn, James M., eds. (1986). *The Correspondence of James Boswell with David Garrick, Edmund Burke, and Edmond Malone*. New York: McGraw-Hill.

Barchas, Janine (2003). *Graphic Design, Print Culture, and the Eighteenth-Century Novel*. Cambridge: Cambridge University Press.

Bonnell, Thomas F. (2012). *James Boswell's* Life of Johnson: *An Edition of the Original Manuscript in Four Volumes. Volume 3: 1776–1780*. Edinburgh: Edinburgh University Press.

Bonnell, Thomas F. (2019). *James Boswell's* Life of Johnson: *An Edition of the Original Manuscript in Four Volumes. Volume 4: 1780–1784*. Edinburgh: Edinburgh University Press.

Boswell, James (1768). *An Account of Corsica, the Journal of a Tour to That Island; and Memoirs of Pascal Paoli*. Glasgow: Edward & Charles Dilly.

Boswell, James (1785). *The Journal of a Tour to the Hebrides, with Samuel Johnson, LL.D*. London: Charles Dilly (2nd ed., 1785; 3rd ed., 1786).

Boswell, James (1790a [i.e., 1791]). *The Celebrated Letter from Samuel Johnson, LL.D. to Philip Dormer Stanhope, Earl of Chesterfield; Now First Published, with Notes*. London: Charles Dilly.

Boswell, James (1790b [i.e., 1791]). *A Conversation between His Most Sacred Majesty George III. and Samuel Johnson, LL.D. Illustrated with Observations*. London: Charles Dilly.

Boswell, James (1791a). *No Abolition of Slavery; or the Universal Empire of Love: A Poem*. London: R. Faulder.

Boswell, James (1791b). *The Life of Samuel Johnson, LL.D*. London: Charles Dilly.

Boswell, James (1792). *The Life of Samuel Johnson, LL.D*. Dublin: R. Cross & eleven others, including P. Byrne.

Boswell, James (1793). *The Life of Samuel Johnson, LL.D.*, 2nd ed. London: Charles Dilly.

Boswell, James (1799). *The Life of Samuel Johnson, LL.D.*, 3rd ed. London: Charles Dilly.

Boswell, James (1831). *The Life of Samuel Johnson*, ed. John Wilson Croker, 5 vols. London: John Murray.

Boswell, James (1998). *Life of Johnson*, ed. R. W. Chapman. Introduced by Pat Rogers. Oxford: Oxford World's Classics.

Boswell, James (2008). *The Life of Samuel Johnson*, ed. David Womersley. London: Penguin Classics.

Boswell, James (2010). *London Journal, 1762–1763*, ed. Gordon Turnbull. London: Penguin Classics.

Brady, Frank (1984). *James Boswell: The Later Years, 1769–1795*. New York: McGraw-Hill.

Brown, Anthony E. (1991). *Boswellian Studies: A Bibliography*, 3rd ed. Edinburgh: Edinburgh University Press.

Brown, Stephen W. & McDougall, Warren, eds. (2012). *The Edinburgh History of the Book in Scotland. Volume 2: Enlightenment and Expansion, 1707–1800*. Edinburgh: Edinburgh University Press.

Buchanan, David (1974). *The Treasure of Auchinleck: The Story of the Boswell Papers*. New York: McGraw-Hill.

Chapman, R. W. (1928). Boswell's Revises of the *Life of Johnson*. In David Nichol Smith, R. W. Chapman & L. F. Powell, *Johnson and Boswell Revised by Themselves and Others*. Oxford: Clarendon Press, pp. 21–50.

Clingham, Greg (2017). John Opie's Portraits of Dr. Johnson. *Harvard Library Bulletin*, 28(2), 57–80.

Cole, Richard Cargill (1986). *Irish Booksellers and English Writers, 1740–1800*. London: Mansell.

Courtenay, John (1786a). *A Poetical Review of the Literary and Moral Character of the Late Samuel Johnson, L.L.D*. London: Charles Dilly.

Courtenay, John (1786b). *A Poetical Review of the Literary and Moral Character of the Late Samuel Johnson, LL.D.*, 3rd ed. London: Charles Dilly.

Czennia, Bärbel & Clingham, Greg, eds. (2021). *Oriental Networks: Culture, Commerce, and Communication in the Long Eighteenth Century.* Lewisburg, PA: Bucknell University Press.

Danziger, Marlies K. & Brady, Frank, eds. (1989). *Boswell: The Great Biographer, 1789–1795.* New York: McGraw-Hill.

Darnton, Robert (1979). *The Business of Enlightenment: A Publishing History of the* Encyclopédie, *1775–1800.* Cambridge, MA: Harvard University Press.

[Dilly, Charles] (1787). *A Catalogue of Books Printed for, and Sold by Charles Dilly, in London.* London: Charles Dilly.

Downie, J. A. (2013). Printing for the Author in the Long Eighteenth Century. In Sandro Jung, ed., *British Literature and Print Culture.* Cambridge: D. S. Brewer, pp. 58–77.

Edmondson, Chloe & Edelstein, Dan, eds. (2019). *Networks of Enlightenment: Digital Approaches to the Republic of Letters.* Liverpool: Liverpool University Press.

Farington, Joseph (1978–84). *The Diary of Joseph Farington*, ed. Kenneth Garlick, Angus Macintyre & Kathryn Cave, 16 vols. New Haven, CT: Yale University Press.

Feather, John (1985). *The Provincial Book Trade in Eighteenth-Century England.* Cambridge: Cambridge University Press.

Fifer, Charles N., ed. (1976). *The Correspondence of James Boswell with Certain Members of the Club.* New York: McGraw-Hill.

Fleeman, J. D. (2000). *A Bibliography of the Works of Samuel Johnson*, 2 vols. Oxford: Clarendon Press.

Flint, Christopher (2011). *The Appearance of Print in Eighteenth-Century Fiction.* Cambridge: Cambridge University Press.

Folkenflik, Robert (2014). Blinking Sam, "Surly Sam," and "Johnson's Grimly Ghost." In Howard D. Weinbrot, ed., *Samuel Johnson: New Contexts for a New Century.* San Marino, CA: Huntington Library, pp. 265–311.

Gaskell, Philip (1986). *A Bibliography of the Foulis Press*, 2nd ed. Winchester: St. Paul's Bibliographies.

Gaskell, Philip (1995). *A New Introduction to Bibliography*, 2nd ed. Winchester: St. Paul's Bibliographies.

Gies, David T. & Wall, Cynthia, eds. (2018). *The Eighteenth Centuries: Global Networks of Enlightenment.* Charlottesville: University of Virginia Press.

Griffiths, D. M. (2004). Baldwin Family. *Oxford Dictionary of National Biography.* Oxford: Oxford University Press.

Gross, Robert A. & Kelley, Mary, eds. (2010). *A History of the Book in America. Volume 2: An Extensive Republic. Print, Culture, and Society in the New Nation, 1790–1840.* Chapel Hill: University of North Carolina Press.

Grundy, Isobel (2009). Women and Print: Readers, Writers and the Market. In Michael F. Suarez & Michael L. Turner, eds., *The Cambridge History of the Book in Britain. Volume 5: 1695–1830.* Cambridge: Cambridge University Press, pp. 146–59.

Hart, Edward (1952). The Contributions of John Nichols to Boswell's *Life of Johnson. PMLA*, 67(4), 391–410.

Hawkins, Sir John (1787). *The Life of Samuel Johnson.* London: J. Buckland and forty others, including J. Rivington & Sons, J. Robson, C. Dilly, G. J. & J. Robinson, T. Cadell, J. Nichols, R. Baldwin, R. Faulder & A. Strahan.

Heath, John (1993). *The Heath Family Engravers, 1779–1878. Volume 1: James Heath.* Aldershot: Scolar Press.

Henry, Robert (1771–93). *The History of Great Britain*, 6 vols. London & Edinburgh: Printed for the Author.

Hill, George Birkbeck, & Powell, L. F., eds. (1934–64). *Boswell's* Life of Johnson. *Together with Boswell's* Journal of a Tour to the Hebrides *and Johnson's* Diary of a Journey into North Wales, 6 vols. Oxford: Oxford University Press. Abbreviated in references as *Life*.

Hill, Jonathan E. (1999). From Provisional to Permanent: Books in Boards, 1790–1840. *The Library*, 21(3), 247–73.

Hinks, John, & Feely, Catherine, eds. (2017). *Historical Networks in the Book Trade.* London: Routledge.

Horne, Colin J. (1950). Boswell and Literary Property. *Notes & Queries*, 195, 296–98.

Johnson, Samuel (1755). *A Dictionary of the English Language*, 2 vols. London, J. & P. Knapton, T. & T. Longman, C. Hitch & L. Hawes, A. Millar, R. & J. Dodsley.

Johnson, Samuel (1786). *A Dictionary of the English Language.* London: Harrison & Company.

Kairoff, Claudia Thomas (2012). *Anna Seward and the End of the Eighteenth Century.* Baltimore, MD: Johns Hopkins University Press.

Lambert, Elizabeth (1998). Boswell's Burke: The Literary Consequences of Ambivalence, *Age of Johnson*, 9, 201–35.

Larsen, Lyle, ed. (2008). *James Boswell: As His Contemporaries Saw Him.* Madison, NJ: Fairleigh Dickinson University Press.

Life. See Hill, George Birkbeck, & Powell, L. F. (1934–64), vols. 1–4.

Lustig, Irma S. (1972). Boswell at Work: The "Animadversions" on Mrs. Piozzi. *Modern Language Review*, 67(1), 11–30.

Lustig, Irma S. (1977). The Compiler of *Dr. Johnson's Table Talk*, 1785. *Papers of the Bibliographical Society of America*, 71, 83–88.

Lustig, Irma S. (1987). Facts and Deductions: The Curious History of Reynolds's First Portrait of Johnson, 1756. *Age of Johnson*, 1, 161–80.

Lustig, Irma S. & Pottle, Frederick A., eds. (1986). *Boswell: The English Experiment, 1785–1789*. New York: McGraw-Hill.

Macaulay, Thomas Babington (August–December 1831). Review of John Wilson Croker's edition of Boswell's *Life of Johnson*, *Edinburgh Review*, 54, 1–38.

Mannings, David (2000). *Sir Joshua Reynolds: A Complete Catalogue of His Paintings*, 2 vols. New Haven, CT: Yale University Press.

Maxted, Ian (1977). *The London Book Trades, 1775–1800: A Preliminary Checklist of Members*. Folkestone, UK: Dawson.

[McDonnell, David Evans] (1785). *Dr. Johnson's Table Talk: or, Conversations of the Late Samuel Johnson, L.L.D. on a Variety of Useful and Entertaining Subjects*. London: G. G. J. & J. Robinson.

McGowan, Ian (1996). Boswell at Work: The Revision and Publication of *The Journal of a Tour to the Hebrides*. In Alvaro Ribeiro & James G. Basker, eds., *Tradition in Transition: Women Writers, Marginal Texts, and the Eighteenth-Century Canon*. Oxford: Clarendon Press, pp. 127–43.

McKenzie, D. F. (1999). *Bibliography and the Sociology of Texts*. Cambridge: Cambridge University Press.

McKenzie, D. F. (2002). Typography and Meaning: The Case of William Congreve. In Peter D. MacDonald & Michael F. Suarez, eds., *Making Meaning: "Printers of the Mind" and Other Essays*. Amherst: University of Massachusetts Press, ch. 8.

Mee, Jon, ed. (2015). Special issue on Networks of Improvement. *Journal for Eighteenth-Century Studies* 38(4).

Montagu, Elizabeth (1769). *An Essay on the Writings and Genius of Shakespear*. London: J. Dodsley, Baker & Leigh, J. Walter, T. Cadell & J. Wilkie.

Nichols, John & Nichols, John Bowyer (1817–58). *Illustrations of the Literary History of the Eighteenth Century*, 8 vols. London: Nichols.

Pindar, Peter [Wolcot, John] (1786). *A Poetical and Congratulatory Epistle to James Boswell, Esq. on His Journal of a Tour to the Hebrides, with the Celebrated Dr. Johnson*. London: G. Kearsley.

Piozzi, Hester Lynch (1786). *Anecdotes of the Late Samuel Johnson, LL.D. during the Last Twenty Years of His Life*. London: T. Cadell.

Pooley, Julian (2011). "Conciliating His Esteem": John Nichols's Contribution to Johnson's *Lives of the Poets*, to Biographies of Johnson, and to Later Johnsonian Scholarship. *Age of Johnson*, 21, 143–92.

Pottle, Frederick A. (1929). *The Literary Career of James Boswell, Esq.* Oxford: Clarendon Press.

Pottle, Frederick A. (1966). *Boswell: The Earlier Years, 1740–1769.* New York: McGraw-Hill.

Pottle, Frederick A. (1971). James Boswell, 1740–95. In George Watson, ed., *The New Cambridge Bibliography of English Literature. Volume 2: 1660–1800.* Cambridge: Cambridge University Press, pp. 1210–49.

Pottle, Frederick A. (1982). *Pride and Negligence: The History of the Boswell Papers.* New York: McGraw-Hill.

Pottle, Marion S., Abbott, Claude Colleer & Pottle, Frederick A., eds. (1993). *Catalogue of the Papers of James Boswell at Yale University*, 3 vols. Edinburgh: Edinburgh University Press.

Powell, L. F. (1928). The Revision of Dr. Birkbeck Hill's Boswell. In David Nichol Smith, R. W. Chapman & L. F. Powell, *Johnson and Boswell Revised by Themselves and Others.* Oxford: Clarendon Press, pp. 53–66.

Purdie, D. W. & Gow, N. (2002). The Maladies of James Boswell, Advocate. *Journal of the Royal College of Physicians of Edinburgh*, 32, 197–202.

Raven, James (2007). *The Business of Books: Booksellers and the English Book Trade.* New Haven, CT: Yale University Press.

Raven, James (2014). *Bookscape: Geographies of Printing and Publishing in London before 1800.* London: The British Library.

Redford, Bruce, ed. (1992–4). *The Letters of Samuel Johnson*, 5 vols. Princeton, NJ: Princeton University Press.

Redford, Bruce (2002). *Designing the* Life of Johnson. Oxford: Oxford University Press.

Redford, Bruce, with Goldring, Elizabeth, eds. (1998). *James Boswell's* Life of Johnson*: An Edition of the Original Manuscript in Four Volumes. Volume 2: 1766–1776.* Edinburgh: Edinburgh University Press.

Rowlandson, Thomas (1786). *Picturesque Beauties of Boswell.* London.

Schellenberg, Betty A. (2016). *Literary Coteries and the Making of Modern Print Culture, 1740–1790.* Cambridge: Cambridge University Press.

Scott, Geoffrey, & Pottle, Frederick A., eds. (1928–34). *Private Papers of James Boswell from Malahide Castle*, 18 vols. Mt. Vernon, NY: privately printed.

Serrat, Francesca Blanch (2019). "I mourn their nature, but admire their art": Anna Seward's Assertion of Critical Authority in Maturity and Old Age. *ES Review*, 40, 11–31.

Seymour, Terry I. (2016). *Boswell's Books: Four Generations of Collecting and Collectors.* New Castle, DE: Oak Knoll Press.

Sher, Richard B. (1998). Corporatism and Consensus in the Late Eighteenth-Century Book Trade: The Edinburgh Booksellers' Society in Comparative Perspective, *Book History*, 1, 32–90.

Sher, Richard B. (1999). William Buchan's *Domestic Medicine*: Laying Book History Open. In Peter Isaac & Barry McKay, eds., *The Human Face of the Book Trade: Print Culture and Its Creators*. Winchester, UK: St. Paul's Bibliographies, pp. 45–64.

Sher, Richard B. (2004). New Light on the Publication and Reception of *The Wealth of Nations*. *Adam Smith Review*, 1, 3–29.

Sher, Richard B. (2006). *The Enlightenment and the Book: Scottish Authors and Their Publishers in Eighteenth-Century Britain, Ireland, and America*. Chicago: University of Chicago Press.

Sher, Richard B., ed. (2022). *The Correspondence of James Boswell and Sir William Forbes of Pitsligo*. Edinburgh: Edinburgh University Press.

Sher, Richard B. (forthcoming). Sir William Forbes of Pitsligo and Boswell's Life of Johnson. In Greg Clingham, ed., *Boswell's Life of Johnson, 1791–2021: Book, Biography, Criticism*. Newark, DE: University of Delaware Press.

Sherbo, Arthur (1989). *Isaac Reed, Editoria Factotum*. Victoria: University of Victoria.

Sisman, Adam (2002). *Boswell's Presumptuous Task: The Making of the Life of Dr. Johnson*. London: Penguin Books.

Suarez, Michael F. & Turner, Michael L., eds. (2009). *The Cambridge History of the Book in Britain. Volume 5: 1695–1830*. Cambridge: Cambridge University Press.

Tankard, Paul (2012). Boswell, George Steevens, and the Johnsonian Biography Wars. *Age of Johnson*, 22, 73–95.

Tankard, Paul, ed. (2014). *Facts and Inventions: Selections from the Journalism of James Boswell*. New Haven, CT: Yale University Press.

Tankard, Paul (2021). Anonymity and the Press: The Case of Boswell. In Donald J. Newman, ed., *Boswell and the Press: Essays on the Ephemeral Writing of James Boswell*. Lewisburg, PA: Bucknell University Press, pp. 32–48.

Taylor, John (1832). *Records of My Life*, 2 vols. London: Edward Bull.

Thomas, F. [pseud.] (1792). *The Life of Dr. Samuel Johnson, LL.D., Carefully Abridged from Mr. Boswell's Large Work*. London: Printed for the Editor.

Tinker, Chauncey Brewster, ed. (1924). *Letters of James Boswell*, 2 vols. Oxford: Clarendon Press.

Tour. See Hill, George Birkbeck, & Powell, L. F. (1934–64), vol. 5.

Towsey, Mark (2019). *Reading History in Britain and America, c.1750–c.1840*. Cambridge: Cambridge University Press.

Waingrow, Marshall, ed. (1994). *James Boswell's* Life of Johnson*: An Edition of the Original Manuscript in Four Volumes. Volume 1: 1709–1765*. Edinburgh: Edinburgh University Press.

Waingrow, Marshall, ed. (2001). *The Correspondence and Other Papers of James Boswell Relating to the Making of the* Life of Johnson, 2nd ed. Edinburgh: Edinburgh University Press.

Wendorf, Richard (2022). *Printing History and Cultural Change: Fashioning the Modern English Text in Eighteenth-Century Britain*. Oxford: Oxford University Press.

Werkmeister, Lucyle (1963). *Jemmie Boswell and the London Daily Press, 1785–1795*. New York: New York Public Library.

Williams, Helen (2021). *Laurence Sterne and the Eighteenth-Century Book*. Cambridge: Cambridge University Press.

Yung, Kai Kin (1984). *Samuel Johnson, 1709–84*. London: Arts Council of Great Britain.

Unpublished Documents and Online Resources

ESTC: English Short-Title Catalogue, British Library, http://estc.bl.uk.

Fettercairn Papers (papers of Sir William Forbes of Pitsligo & family), National Library of Scotland, Acc. 4796.

Hamilton & Company (1794), circular, Records of Bell & Bradfute, Edinburgh City Archives, SL 138/9.

Harvard University, Houghton Library, Donald & Mary Hyde Collection of Dr. Samuel Johnson (& other collections).

Heath ARA: James Heath, ARA (1757–1834), Royal Academy of Arts, www .royalacademy.org.uk/art-artists/name/james-heath-ara.

NPG: National Portrait Gallery. NPG 1597: Dr Samuel Johnson by Sir Joshua Reynolds, www.npg.org.uk/collections/research/programmes/conservation/ & www.npg.org.uk/collections/search/portrait/mw03491/Samuel-Johnson; NPG D34873: Dr Samuel Johnson by James Heath, https://npg.org.uk/collections/ search/portrait-list.php?search=sp&sText=D34873&firstRun=true.

Seventeenth and Eighteenth Century Burney Newspapers Collection (Gale), from the British Library, accessed online via Rutgers University, https://gale .com/c/seventeenth-and-eighteenth-century-burney-newspapers-collection.

Seymour, Terry (2021). "Principal Corrections and Additions" to *Boswell's Books* (privately circulated).

Stationers' Company Archive, London, Stationers' Register.

Times: *The Times* Digital Archive, 1785–2014 (Gale), accessed online via Rutgers University, https://gale.com/c/the-times-digital-archive.

Yale: Yale University, Beinecke Rare Book and Manuscript Library, The Boswell Collection, GEN MSS 89. Many of the following manuscripts are accessible online at https://beinecke.library.yale.edu/collections/highlights/boswell-collection. They are cited in this work with the following reference letters (see Pottle, Abbott & Pottle, 1993):

A=Accounts & Other Financial Papers. A 52: general financial statements. A 59–A 64: accounts & financial documents relating to the first two editions of the *Life*.

C=Letters to James Boswell & Others.

J=Journal: All references to Boswell's journal are quoted from the original manuscripts, accessible online. Edited versions of the text can be found in the published trade edition of Boswell's journal.

L=Letters Written by James Boswell.

M=Manuscripts. M 38: Boswelliana; M 145: *Life* Manuscript, Papers Apart; M 251–255: Boswell's Register of Letters, Sent and Received, 1763–90.

P=Printed Matter & Other Non-Manuscript Material. P 100, 100.1, & 101: newspaper cuttings relating to the *Life*.

Acknowledgments

I wish to thank Tom Bonnell, Andy Heisel, Terry Seymour, Doris Sher, and especially Gordon Turnbull, Bill Zachs, and an anonymous press reviewer for their helpful readings of earlier drafts. Thanks also to the series editors, Eve Bannet and Markman Ellis; Bethany Thomas and Adam Hooper at Cambridge University Press; and Jim Caudle, Greg Clingham, Andy Heisel, Kevin Marshall, Julian Pooley, Paul Tankard, and David Whitesell for their assistance with various aspects of this work. For the illustrations and permission to publish them, my primary debt is to Andy Heisel and the Beinecke Rare Book and Manuscript Library at Yale University; I am also grateful to the Houghton Library at Harvard University (John Overholt), the National Library of Scotland (Ralph McLean), the Stationers' Company (Ruth Frendo and Gabby Price), the Heath-Caldwell Family Archive (J. J. Heath-Caldwell), Gale Publishing (Regina Ambrosino and Rita Barvais), and the Terry I. Seymour Collection (Terry Seymour and Kassie Seymour).

Cambridge Elements ☰

Eighteenth-Century Connections

Series Editors

Eve Tavor Bannet
University of Oklahoma

Eve Tavor Bannet is George Lynn Cross Professor Emeritus, University of Oklahoma and editor of *Studies in Eighteenth-Century Culture*. Her monographs include *Empire of Letters: Letter Manuals and Transatlantic Correspondence 1688–1820* (Cambridge, 2005), *Transatlantic Stories and the History of Reading, 1720–1820* (Cambridge, 2011), and *Eighteenth-Century Manners of Reading: Print Culture and Popular Instruction in the Anglophone Atlantic World* (Cambridge, 2017). She is editor of *British and American Letter Manuals 1680–1810* (Pickering & Chatto, 2008), *Emma Corbett* (Broadview, 2011) and, with Susan Manning, *Transatlantic Literary Studies* (Cambridge, 2012).

Markman Ellis
Queen Mary University of London

Markman Ellis is Professor of Eighteenth-Century Studies at Queen Mary University of London. He is the author of *The Politics of Sensibility: Race, Gender and Commerce in the Sentimental Novel* (1996), *The History of Gothic Fiction* (2000), *The Coffee-House: a Cultural History* (2004), and *Empire of Tea* (co-authored, 2015). He edited *Eighteenth-Century Coffee-House Culture* (4 vols, 2006) and *Tea and the Tea-Table in Eighteenth-Century England* (4 vols, 2010), and co-editor of *Discourses of Slavery and Abolition* (2004) and *Prostitution and Eighteenth-Century Culture: Sex, Commerce and Morality* (2012).

Advisory Board

Linda Bree, *Independent*
Claire Connolly, *University College Cork*
Gillian Dow, *University of Southampton*
James Harris, *University of St Andrews*
Thomas Keymer, *University of Toronto*
Jon Mee, *University of York*
Carla Mulford, *Penn State University*
Nicola Parsons, *University of Sydney*
Manushag Powell, *Purdue University*
Robbie Richardson, *University of Kent*
Shef Rogers, *University of Otago*
Eleanor Shevlin, *West Chester University*
David Taylor, *Oxford University*
Chloe Wigston Smith, *University of York*
Roxann Wheeler, *Ohio State University*
Eugenia Zuroski, *MacMaster University*

About the Series

Exploring connections between verbal and visual texts and the people, networks, cultures and places that engendered and enjoyed them during the long Eighteenth Century, this innovative series also examines the period's uses of oral, written and visual media, and experiments with the digital platform to facilitate communication of original scholarship with both colleagues and students.

Cambridge Elements ⹀

Eighteenth-Century Connections

A full series listing is available at: www.cambridge.org/EECC

Printed in the United States
by Baker & Taylor Publisher Services